The Man Who Refused Heaven

The Man Who Refused Heaven

*The Humor of
Paramhansa Yogananda*

Paramhansa Yogananda
Swami Kriyananda

Crystal Clarity Publishers
Nevada City, California

Crystal Clarity Publishers, Nevada City, CA 95959
Copyright © 2017 by Hansa Trust
All rights reserved. Published 2017

Paperback ISBN: 978-1-56589-311-5
ePub ISBN: 978-1-56589-571-3

Printed in China
1 3 5 7 9 10 8 6 4 2

Cover and interior design by Tejindra Scott Tully

LIBRARY OF CONGRESS CATALOGING-IN-PUBLICATION DATA

[CIP data block available]

www.crystalclarity.com
clarity@crystalclarity.com
800-424-1055

Contents

Introduction. 9

1. We Are All a Little Bit Crazy and Don't Know It. . 15
2. Laughing at Life's Folly 27
3. Having Fun with People 37
4. Health Is Not Always a Serious Matter 47
5. Doing What Works. 55
6. The Practice of Religion 67
7. Concentration and Meditation 81
8. Stories from His Early Years. 97
9. Training the Disciples. 107
10. Stories with a Moral 121

Appendices 143
About the Author 147
About Ananda and The Expanding Light. 148
Further Explorations 152

The Man Who Refused Heaven

*The Humor of
Paramhansa Yogananda*

INTRODUCTION

O Silent Laughter,
smile Thou through my soul.
Let my soul smile through my heart.
And let my heart smile through my eyes.

O Prince of Smiles,
make me a smile-millionaire,
that I may scatter Thy rich smiles
in sad hearts freely, everywhere!

—*Paramhansa Yogananda*

LAUGHTER IS ONE OF THE GREATEST JOYS IN LIFE. Our hope for this book is that it will bring you laughter and delight. In laughter we touch the joy that lies within waiting to be awakened—the same inner joy that is most deeply experienced by the saints.

Peggy Dietz acted for some years as Yogananda's assistant, often welcoming reporters from Los Angeles newspapers who came to interview the Master. Whenever she asked them, "What characteristics do you appreciate in Yogananda?" they invariably answered, "His love—and his sense of humor!"

In teaching his ministers how to lecture, Yogananda included the following instructions:

Before lecturing, meditate deeply. Then, holding onto that meditative calmness, think about what you intend to say. Write down your ideas. Include one or two funny stories, because people are more receptive if they can enjoy a good laugh.*

Yogananda often quoted the classic Sanskrit definition, given in the eighth century A.D. by the great Hindu teacher Adi Shankaracharya: "God is *Sat-chid-ananda*," which Yogananda translated as, "God is ever-existing, ever-conscious, ever-new bliss."

* From *The New Path* by Swami Kriyananda.

He explained that when God, who is bliss, *became* His creation, then all life had as its essence that same bliss. Thus we see one common thread uniting all people: the search for happiness. Because our essential nature is joy, we will not stop seeking until we find it.

In his mystical poem "Samadhi," Yogananda describes the highest state of consciousness: the soul realizing its oneness with God. This exalted poem ends with these lines:

> *A tiny bubble of laughter, I*
> *Am become the Sea of Mirth Itself.*

Yogananda's experience of life, and his experience of the goal of life, was of divine joy. He lived in joy always, and sought to awaken joy in others. Sometimes he expressed that joy through deep seriousness, when seriousness was called for, but equally through an overflowing merriment and even childlike playfulness.

We have included in this book, not only Yogananda's original words, but also stories about the Master by Swami Kriyananda. Not long after Kriyananda became a disciple of Yogananda in 1948, Yogananda began asking him to take down his words. Kriyananda filled many notebooks with stories the Master liked to tell in public (but had not himself written down), as well as with his own accounts of how Yogananda worked with people and trained his disciples. Kriyananda shares his own personal experiences with the Master, as well as those told to him by other disciples. These stories greatly broaden our experience of the Master's use of humor.

As you read, try to tune in to the wellspring of divine joy from which Yogananda's humor bubbled into expression. Sometimes the Master used humor to express important spiritual principles. Sometimes he used humor in training disciples, or even acquaintances, as a way of giving lessons that reasoned lectures alone could never communicate.

This book is both playful and deep. The deeper message is that God's joy is within us always, ours to experience, and ours to share with others.

—Crystal Clarity Publishers

Chapter *1*

WE ARE ALL A LITTLE BIT CRAZY
AND DON'T KNOW IT

1

WARNER OLAND, the Hollywood actor who played Fu Manchu in that series of movies, and also Charlie Chan in seventeen other movies, was a rather dour man, but he was famous. Yogananda found himself seated opposite him on a train journey. The actor, seeing Yogananda's long hair and orange robe, gave the Master a look of disgust, then turned away.

"Excuse me," the Master said, "why are you wearing that expression?"

"None of your business!" replied the other, rudely.

"Forgive me, but it *is* my business," Yogananda answered. "I have to sit here and look at you! It would be much pleasanter if the expression you wore were not so sour."

"You seem to be a very audacious sort of person," Oland commented with a laugh. "Who are you?"

"That's just the thing!" Yogananda replied. "We have a great opportunity before us today. You know, everyone in the world is a little bit crazy, but no one gets to find out about his own craziness because he mixes only with people whose craziness is of the same kind as his own. I know about your kind of craziness, because I've seen you on the screen, but you don't know about mine. If you can convince me that your way of life is better, then I will become a movie actor. But if I can convince you that my way is better, you ought to follow me."

"Well," Yogananda reported later, "he agreed to my terms, and we talked everything out. And—I never became a movie actor, but he did become my student!"

→2←

AN ORTHODOX MINISTER ONCE, incensed at the presence of an orange-robed "heathen" in this, our most Christian land, and perturbed especially because the Master wouldn't endorse certain of his more narrow dogmas, shouted at him one day on a train, "You will go to hell!"

Master, seeing the anger etched on the man's face, replied affably, "Well, I may get there by and by, but my friend, *you* are there already!" The passengers in the carriage had been following this dialogue with interest. At this answer, there came a general wave of laughter.

→3←

On another occasion, in the Pacific Northwest, Yogananda stopped at a farmhouse hoping to buy some cherries, and got into a discussion on religion with the farmer. At a certain point this man, who proved to be a religious fanatic, shouted, "We are all sinners!—and the Lord will burn our souls in hell-fire and brimstone!"

The Master paused a moment before replying. Then he asked, as if irrelevantly, "You have a son, haven't you?"

The other answered dolefully, "Yes. I have a son."

"He gives you trouble, doesn't he?"

"Oh, my God, what trouble!"

"He drinks, I think?"

"Like a whale! You can't imagine the grief I go through on his account."

Yogananda then announced confidently, "I have a cure for his problem."

"Oh, sir, if you can help me with that, I'll be grateful to you forever!"

"Well, here's what you do: The next time he comes home late at night, drunk . . ." He interrupted himself.

"Have you a large oven?"

The man glared suspiciously. "Say," he demanded, "what have you got in mind?"

"No, no, just wait." Yogananda spoke reassuringly. "I'm offering you a solution to your problem."

Hesitantly the man replied, "Yes, I have such an oven."

"Has it a large door?"

Suddenly again apprehensive, the man cried, "Just a minute! Where is all this heading?"

The Master spoke soothingly. "Just be calm. I'm going to solve everything for you."

The other sat back, relaxing slightly.

"Now then, here's what you do: The next time your son comes home drunk...well, first, have the oven good and hot..."

The man sat up again, horrified.

Yogananda was now speaking hurriedly: "Grab him; tie him up with a strong rope, and shove him into the oven!"

Furiously indignant, the man shouted, "Blasphemer! Evildoer! Whoever heard of a father throwing his own son into an oven! Get out of my house this minute!"

Yogananda then spoke appeasingly. "Don't you understand what I've just said to you? You said God wants to throw us all into hell. But He is our true Father! You, a mere human being, were horrified at the thought of throwing your own son into an oven despite all the trouble he's given you. How could you think the Divine Father, who has infinitely greater love than you, and who created parental love, would burn His own children with hell-fire and brimstone?"

The old man's eyes filled with tears of repentance as he said, "I see now." He reflected a moment. "Yes, you are right." He looked at his visitor with a grateful smile. "Oh, thank you! You've cured me of a serious error. I understand now that the Heavenly Father is a God of love. He *can't* wish our destruction! Thank you! Thank you!"

→4←

A DISCIPLE: "Sir, if a white person is prejudiced against blacks, won't it follow that in his next life he himself will be born black?"

Paramhansa Yogananda laughed. "That's perfectly true! Aversion is just as strong a magnetic force as attraction.

"God is not impressed by human prejudices.

"Sometimes," he continued, "you see whole families who do nothing but fight amongst themselves. They were enemies before—attracted together into the same home, where now they must work out their hatred at close quarters!

"There is the story of a church in one of the southern states of America. It was a place where only white people were allowed to attend the services.

"Jim, the Negro janitor, wanted more than anything else to be permitted to worship with the congregation on Sunday mornings. 'Jim,' the minister explained to him, 'I'd love to have you join us. But if you did so, you know I'd lose my job.'

"One night Jim prayed broken-heartedly to Jesus, 'Lord, why can't I worship in there with the white folk?' After some time he fell asleep, and a vision was granted him: Jesus Christ appeared in a great light, smiling compassionately.

"'My son,' Jesus said, 'don't feel too badly. For twenty years I've been trying to enter that very church myself, and I haven't yet succeeded!'"

→5←

ONCE UPON A TIME a violently dogmatic Hindu priest presided over a temple, and expected unquestioning obedience from his disciples. The ignorant priest was magnetic enough to attract a group of assorted illiterates who did nothing but agree with him.

One day his students asked, "Honored Sir, will you please show us the absolutely certain method of contacting God?"

The priest replied, "My loyal children, I can teach you how to contact God—as long as you do exactly as I do."

"Hallelujah! Blessings on our great teacher! We solemnly swear to do exactly as you do."

The priest sat on a cushion in the middle of the temple with the dogma-stuffed students sitting around him. He braced up and said, "Sit upright." Two hundred devout followers shouted, "Sit upright." The priest, at this unexpected display of idiocy, looked around, and the disciples, seeing the master look around, also looked around.

In disgust, the master-priest sat bolt upright, closed his eyes and prayed, "O Spirit, benign Lord." The disciples all sat upright and shouted in unison, "O Spirit, benign Lord."

The priest exclaimed again, "Benign Lord of the universe, bless us with the knowledge that will make us obey our master implicitly." The students, with increased devotion, together repeated these words.

The priest felt a tickling sensation in his throat and he coughed. The disciples coughed too. The master was aghast. As he coughed again and sneezed, all his disciples violently coughed and sneezed. The master was white with anger and shouted, "Shut up, you idiots! Don't cough, and don't imitate me!" The disciples shouted together, "Shut up, you idiots! Don't cough, and don't imitate me."

The priest, now purple with rage, stood up and shouted at the top of his voice, "This outrageous idiocy must stop." The two hundred products of his training stood up and shouted, "This outrageous idiocy must stop."

Now the priest was beside himself with wrath, and, forgetting the dignity of his position, he forcefully slapped the cheek of one of his assorted idiots. His well-trained two hundred followed suit and slapped one another, including the master, until their cheeks began to burn like fire.

The priest, his body burning like fire from the unending blows, rushed out of the temple crying, "Water, water." The disciples followed him shouting, "Water, water," and slapping one another the whole time.

The master-priest, seeing no other way of escape, jumped into the well to cool his burning cheeks and body. Well, you know what happened then. The two hundred dogma-drugged disciples jumped into the well on top of the master-priest.

Now the priest had kept his promise, for they all went to Heaven together.

This story shows that dogmatists who follow untested beliefs will ultimately, like the blind following the blind, be drowned in the same pit of ignorance. Ignorant students should not cling to ignorant spiritual teachers, for they drag each other down, to sink in ignorance.

Chapter 2

LAUGHING AT LIFE'S FOLLY

→1←

YOGANANDA HAD AN IMPISH, and utterly delightful, sense of humor. This trait may be seen in some of the jokes he told, many of which he'd heard from others.

One was a somewhat left-handed compliment, which he told with a childlike smile: "Your teeth are like stars: they come out at night!"

Another was of three men, an Irishman, an Englishman, and a Scotsman. All three were drinking whiskey when a fly landed in each of their glasses. The Irishman simply sloshed his glass sideways, losing a fair amount of whiskey along with the fly. The Englishman carefully flicked the fly out of the glass. But the Scotsman *squeezed* the fly! I still remember vividly the little touch of glee with which Master uttered that word, *squeezed*.

In still another joke he told, three Scotsmen attended church. As the collection plate was approaching them, one of them fainted, and the other two carried him out.

→ 2 ←

ONE TIME, out of doors at his desert retreat, Master told an amusing story from his early days at the school in Ranchi.

I no longer remember Master's exact words on this occasion. In fact, I couldn't really understand properly what he was saying. He told the story with so much enthusiasm, broad gestures and pantomiming, with laughing expressions and a twinkle in his eyes, that his words became obfuscated. His delight in the story was contagious, however, and I laughed with him delightedly.

→ 3 ←

"THERE WAS A PREACHER many years ago in Harlem," the Master told me. "He was well known as 'Father Divine.' Father Divine once wrote me a letter suggesting that we 'team up.' He signed his letter, 'I am healthy, energetic, and happy in every muscle, bone, molecule, AND ATOM!' Those last two words he underlined vigorously three times. His official chair, I was informed, bore the word 'GOD' carved across the back!" The Master chuckled in amusement at the memory.

→ 4 ←

"People have a very distorted notion of what the spiritual path is all about," Yogananda said. "Visions and phenomena aren't important. What matters is complete self-offering to God. One must be absorbed in His love.

"I remember a man who came forward after a lecture in New York and claimed that he could enter cosmic consciousness at will. Actually, what he meant was that he could travel astrally, but I saw right away that his experiences were imaginary. Still, I couldn't simply tell him so; he wouldn't have believed me. So I invited him up to my room. There I asked him to favor me by going into cosmic consciousness.

"Well, he sat there fidgeting, eyelids flickering, breath heaving—signs, all, of body-consciousness, not of cosmic consciousness! At last he could contain himself no longer.

"'Why don't you ask me where I am?'

"'Well,' I said, to humor him, 'where are you?'

"In rounded tones, as if hallooing from a distance, he replied: 'On top of the dome of the Taj Mahal!'

"'There must be something the matter with your own dome!' I remarked. 'I see you sitting fully here, right in front of me.' He was utterly taken aback.

"I then made a suggestion. 'If you think you can travel all the way to the Taj Mahal in India, why not see if you can go somewhere nearby, to test the validity of your experience?' I suggested that he project himself to the hotel dining room downstairs, and describe what he saw there. He agreed to the test. Going into 'cosmic consciousness' again, he described the dining room as he saw it. He actually believed in his visions, you see. What I wanted to do was demonstrate to him that they were the products of a vivid power of visualization. He described a number of things in the restaurant, including a group of people seated in a corner farther from the door.

"I then described the scene as I saw it. 'In the right-hand corner,' I said, 'there are two women seated at a table by the door.' I described a few more things as they were at the moment. We went downstairs at once, and found the room as I had described it, not as he had. At last he was convinced."

→5←

YOGANANDA FOUND AMUSEMENT in pedantry. He would sometimes joke about its pretensions. A story he liked to tell, laughingly, was the following:

"The wife of a certain philosopher asked him to go out and buy her a bottle of oil. He was returning, later, with the bottle when he began to muse, 'Now, is the oil really in the bottle? Or do my senses deceive me? Could it be, rather, that the bottle is in the oil?'

"His wife met him at the door and demanded, 'Where is the oil?'

"'My wife,' the philosopher declared grandly, 'I have just made an important discovery!'

"'Where is the oil?' she repeated.

"'I am coming to that,' he assured her. 'Listen: I purchased the oil. Then, looking at it, I thought, "Yes, this is oil, and it appears to be inside the bottle. My apperceptive perception, however, doubts whether the oil really is in the bottle, or whether the bottle might not, possibly, be inside the oil."'

"'Where is the oil?' demanded his wife.

"'Yes, yes, I'm just coming to that,' he assured her hastily. 'So then I upturned the bottle. And now, I think that maybe the oil was in the bottle!'

"'You fool!' cried his wife. Picking up a broom, she beat him over his 'apperceptively perceptive' head with it.

"'Now I know,' the philosopher concluded in triumph, 'that the oil was in the bottle!'"

The Master commented, "With real intellectuals, you don't have any trouble. They want the truth, not mere definitions of the truth."

→6←

THE MASTER HAD FUN, sometimes, over the classic "professorial" image.

"There was a philosopher," he said, "who flicked the ash of his cigarette down the back of his wife's dress. 'What are you doing!' she cried indignantly. 'Oh, sorry! sorry!' he replied with a cloudlike smile. 'I thought you were the wall.'"

→7←

The Philosopher and the Boatman

LONG AGO, a learned Hindu philosopher, thoroughly versed in the four vast Hindu Bibles, wanted to cross the holy river Ganges in India. As the humble boatman began to row the philosopher across the river, the proud philosopher thought of showing off his knowledge to the boatman. He asked, "Boatman, have you studied the first Hindu Bible?" The boatman replied, "No sir, I don't know anything about the Hindu Bible." To this the philosopher pityingly remarked, "Mr. Boatman, I must tell you that twenty-five percent of your life is as good as lost."

The boatman swallowed this insult and continued rowing his boat. When the boat had gone some distance across the Ganges, the philosopher's eyes sparkled and he exclaimed loudly, "Mr. Boatman, I must ask you, have you studied the second Hindu Bible?" This roused the boatman and he replied, "Sir, I tell you definitely that I know nothing about the Hindu Bible." To this, the philosopher in cool amusement replied, "Mr. Boatman, I am sorry to tell you that fifty percent of your life is as good as lost."

The boatman angrily settled down to his work at the oars. Now the boat had reached the middle of the river and the wind was blowing fiercely, when the Hindu philosopher's eyes again glistened with superiority and he demanded, "Mr. Boatman, tell me, have you studied the third Hindu Bible?" By this time the boatman was beside himself with anger, and shouted, "Mr. Philosopher, I don't know anything about the Hindu Bibles."

The philosopher, in great, gloating triumph, declared, "Mr. Boatman, I am sorry to tell you that seventy-five percent of your life is as good as lost." The boatman, mumbling to himself, again endured the words of this impossible philosopher.

Ten more minutes passed, when a raging storm lashed the Ganges into huge waves. The boat began to rock like a little leaf in the tumultuous current of the river. The philosopher was trembling, while the boatman with a smile of assurance on his face looked at his passenger and asked, "Mr. Philosopher, you pestered me with so many questions, may I ask you one: Can you swim?" When the trembling philosopher said, "No!" the boatman replied, "Then the whole of your life is lost, my friend, you'll not need those books any more."

The moral of this story is that, no matter how learned or prosperous you are, unless you learn the art of right behavior and right living, you will drown in the sea of difficulty. But, if you know the art of initiating the right actions at the right time, then, with powerful strokes of will power, you can beat all the tests of life and reach the shores of complete contentment.

CHAPTER 3

HAVING FUN WITH PEOPLE

→1←

YOGANANDA'S SYSTEM OF EDUCATION began with the student himself, rather than with the information to be shoveled into his head. Spiritual and moral values should be made attractive by showing that adherence to them brings the happiness that all are seeking.

For instance, at his school in Ranchi (Bihar), there were two boys who fought together constantly. At night, he had them sleep in the same bed! From then on it was constant, sleep-depriving warfare, or enforced peace. They began to show signs of a budding friendship.

Yogananda then, to make sure this new friendship had gone deep enough, tiptoed silently one night to the head of their bed, and stood there. Seeing that they were fast asleep, he reached down and rapped one of them on the forehead. The boy raised himself and spoke angrily to his bedmate.

"Why did you do that?" he demanded.

"What do you mean? I didn't do anything." This answer was so patently sincere that the first boy subsided, too sleepy to wonder how the episode might have occurred.

Once he was soundly asleep, Yogananda leaned down once again and rapped the other boy on the forehead. This boy then sat up and shouted angrily, "I *told* you I didn't do anything!" They both sat up then, ready to do battle, when they happened to glance at the head of the bed. There they saw Yogananda smiling down at them.

"Oh, *you*!" they cried. From that night on they became the best of friends.

→2←

"WOMEN ARE MORE influenced by feeling," the Master used to say, "and men, more by reason. You can see it in the very shape of their bodies. Women's breasts are in the heart region, where the feelings reside. Men's foreheads, on the other hand—the area covering the brain, where the intellect is centered—are square, and often have a slight projection above the eyebrows.

"One day I was talking with a successful woman author. All her life she had been competing in what was primarily a masculine arena, and she prided herself on her intellectual outlook on everything. 'In everything I do,' she told me, 'I am guided entirely by reason.'

"I said nothing. Gradually, however, I steered the conversation around to another woman author—this woman's 'competitor.' When it came to discussing this 'trade rival,' the woman had nothing good to say.

"'Aha,' I said teasingly, 'you go only by reason, do you?' She saw immediately what I meant, and we had a good laugh over it."

→3←

ONE DAY, IN CHICAGO, a drunken stranger staggered up and embraced Yogananda affectionately.

"Hello there, Jeshush Chrisht!"

Master smiled. Then, to give the man a taste of the infinitely better "spirits" he himself enjoyed, he looked deeply into the man's eyes and gave him a taste of divine joy.

"Shay," the fellow cried thickly, "whad're *you* drink'n'?"

The Master replied, his eyes twinkling, "Let's just say, it has a lot of kick in it!" The man was sobered by this glance. "I left him," Master told us later, "wondering what had happened!"

→ 4 ←

"A STUDENT OF THIS WORK in Boston told me he wanted to be a renunciate. I said to him, 'Your path is marriage.'

"'Oh, no!' he vowed, 'I'll *never* marry!' Well, a week later he met a beautiful girl and swore to me that he was deeply in love with her!

"'She isn't the one for you,' I warned him.

"'Oh, but she *is*!' he cried. 'She is my soul mate.'

"Well, it wasn't long after that that he returned shamefacedly. 'I want to be a renunciate,' he announced fervently once again. The girl had left him, having enjoyed spending his money.

"'You have yet to meet the right one,' I said.

"Some time later he told me laughingly of a fat, quite unattractive-looking girl who had been showing an unwelcome interest in him.

"'Aha,' I said, 'this sounds like the right one!'

"'No, Swami, no!' he cried, horrified. 'You were right before. *Please* don't be right this time!'

"'She sounds like the right one for you.'

"It took him some time, but gradually he discovered what a good nature the girl had beneath her unglamorous exterior, and fell deeply in love with her. Eventually they were married."

→5←

"People are so often blinded by outward appearances," Master continued. "Marriage in this country is often a union between a pretty shade of lipstick and a smart-looking bow tie! They hear a little music, fall into a romantic mood, and end up pledging their lives away."

→6←

Yogananda used to say, "People say that women are weaker than men, but a woman with a six-inch tongue can kill a man six feet tall!"

→7←

If you are suffering from the indigestion of unkindness or choleric crabbiness, drink the medicine of sweetness.

→8←

EVERY TIME YOU SEE sad faces, shoot the buckshot of smiles at them. Every time somebody's heart of sorrow is pierced with the bullet of your smile, you have "hit the bull's eye." Every day do target practice by shooting smiles wherever you see sadness.

→9←

The Man Who Refused Heaven

LONG AGO, there lived in India a holy man who spent his days on the peaceful banks of the holy river Ganges. Though troubled by undesirable thoughts, he one day vowed, "I will not stop praying until I find peace during meditation." At the end of three hours, the disturbing thoughts vanished from his temple of meditation, and in their stead he beheld a vision of a beautiful saint standing before him.

This saint spoke with celestial softness, "According to the decree of your past actions, it is metaphysically ordained that at death you will have to choose between living in Heaven with ten fools, or living in Hades with one wise man. Which do you prefer?"

The spiritual aspirant replied, "I prefer to live in Hades with one wise man, for I know from experience that ten fools would make a Hades of Heaven. But I believe that if I were with one real wise man, even in the stygian darkness of Hades, he would help me create Heaven there."

So, if you have a heavenly home but are constantly fighting with your family and friends, you are living in a self-created Hades. On the other hand, even if you live in inharmonious surroundings, if you meditate for a few minutes every day and live in harmony, you will carry your own portable paradise within you wherever you go.

CHAPTER *4*

HEALTH IS NOT ALWAYS
A SERIOUS MATTER

→ 1 ←

OFTEN I AM TOLD by someone struggling with his health, "Oh, asthma, (or tuberculosis or diabetes) runs in my family." I do not need to be told further of his self-hypnotic resignation to an identical doom. But this, dear students, is NOT the way to Truth; it is a jellyfish philosophy. What IS true is that if you continue to live as your father did, you may expect to follow in his footsteps.

I do not say that it is easy to change. Like everything else worth attaining, you must WORK for it! But there is a saying that "any old fish can float downstream, but it takes a *live* one to swim upstream." It is the individual's job to free himself from the shackles of undesirable hereditary tendencies, whether habits of thought, or habits of ill health.

→ 2 ←

The "Worry Fast"

IF YOU ARE SUFFERING from mental ill health, go on a mental diet. A health-giving mental fast will clear the mind and rid it of the accumulated mental poisons resulting from a careless, faulty mental diet. First of all, learn to remove the cause of your worries without permitting them to worry you. Do not feed your mind with daily created mental poisons of fresh worries.

Worries are often the result of attempting to do too many things hurriedly. Do not "bolt" your mental duties, but thoroughly masticate them, one at a time, with the teeth of attention, and saturate them with the saliva of good judgment. Thus you will avoid worry indigestion.

Go on worry fasts. Three times a day, shake off all worries. At seven o'clock in the morning, say to yourself, "All my worries of the night are cast out, and from seven to eight a.m. I refuse to worry, no matter how troublesome are the duties ahead of me. I am on a worry fast." From noon to one p.m., say, "I am cheerful, I will not worry." In the evening, between six and nine o'clock, while in the company of your spouse or hard-to-get-along-with relatives or friends, mentally make a strong resolution, "Within these three hours I will not worry. I refuse to get vexed, even if I am nagged. No matter how tempting it is to indulge in a worry feast, I will resist the temptation." After you succeed in carrying out worry fasts during certain hours of the day, try fasting for one or two weeks at a time. Then, try to prevent the accumulation of worry poisons in your system entirely.

Worry fasting is the negative method for overcoming worry poisoning. There is also a positive method: One infected with the germs of worry must feast frugally, but regularly, on the society of joyful minds. There are some people the song of whose laughter nothing can still. Seek them out, and feast with them on this most vitalizing food of joy. Steadfastly continue your laughter diet, and at the end of a month or two you will see the change—your mind will be filled with sunshine.

→ **3** ←

COULD YOU FOLLOW a musical score, read, walk, write, talk, and meditate simultaneously, doing justice to them all? Well, that is just about what the digestive organs are called on to do three times a day, year in and year out, with an incompatible conglomeration of food-stuffs tossed into their apparatus.

There are five separate digestive fluids in the body, designed to handle the variety of foods we need. The confusion that takes place internally when too many different foods are foisted on an overtaxed "public servant" might be compared to that caused when the manager of a big manufacturing plant issues conflicting orders to the various departments.

When eyes and palate dictate how we nourish this physical temple, to the exclusion of the laws that *should* govern it, there is little wonder that our population fills an increasing number of hospitals.

→4←

IF YOU HAVEN'T ENOUGH will power, try to develop "won't" power. When you are at the dinner table and Mr. Greed tries to chloroform your self-control and lure you to eat more than you should, watch yourself. After partaking of the right quality and quantity of food, say to yourself, "I won't eat any more," and get up from the table and run. When somebody calls, "John, come back. Don't forget the delicious apple pie," just call back, "I won't."

→5←

SOME TIME AGO a man suffering from a chronic nervous heart came to me for healing. He said, "I have tried many things, but I am unable to get rid of my heart trouble."

After calm, intuitive reflection, I told him to bring me a pair of scissors. Alarmed and suspicious, he stared at me, and remonstrated, "Sir, are you going to perform an incision on my heart?!" I laughed and replied, "I am not a doctor, and you have never heard of anyone using scissors for operating upon the heart."

When he reluctantly brought the scissors, I cut off one of his vest buttons and told him not to replace the button and not to touch the place where the missing button belonged. I asked him to come back after fifteen days, and told him I expected him to be healed by that time.

The man laughingly exclaimed, "I will do what you say since I believe in you, but of all the crazy cures, I think this is the craziest."

After fifteen days he came to me, shouting with joy, and said, "The specialists say I am healed of my nervous heart. Sir, what did you do? Did you dispossess the button of a ghost?"

With a smile I said, "Yes, I did! Your hand was constantly fiddling with the vest button near your heart. This button was the 'ghost' nagging your heart into a nervous fit. Your heart, freed from the disturbing vest button, has ceased to trouble you."

→6←

KNOW THAT ANYTHING others do, you can do also. Once I was having dinner with friends. Everything went well until the Roquefort cheese was served. In India we eat only freshly made cheese, so I viewed the little green specks of mold in the cheese with great suspicion. My soul rebelled against it, and my brain cells warned me to have nothing to do with it. But as I looked at my American friends eating the cheese, I mustered courage and took a lump of it into my mouth.

No sooner had it landed there than all the aristocratic delicacies that had preceded it rebelled. There was great clamor and commotion within me, and they let me know that if "Mr. Roquefort" joined them in the stomach, they would all leave the body. I dared not open my mouth, but just nodded in answer to my host's question of whether I liked the cheese!

Then, as I looked intently at the faces of my friends eating Roquefort cheese pleasantly, I suddenly made up my mind. Concentrating deeply, I told my brain cells, "I am your boss; you are my servants. You shall obey me—this foolishness must stop." The next minute I was enjoying "Mr. Roquefort's" company pleasantly, and now he always receives a warm welcome when he enters my "hall of digestion."

CHAPTER 5

DOING WHAT WORKS

→ 1 ←

MASTER OFTEN SAID, "He is happiest who gives everything to God." He told us an amusing story to illustrate his own preference for simple living, free of all ostentation.

"A wealthy student of mine wanted to buy me a new overcoat. Taking me into a well-known clothing store, he invited me to select any coat I wanted. Seeing one that looked nice, I reached out to touch it. But then, seeing the price tag, I quickly withdrew my hand. The coat was very expensive.

"'But I'd be *happy* to buy it for you,' my friend insisted. He added an expensive hat to match. I appreciated his kindness in giving me these gifts. But whenever I wore them, I felt uncomfortable. Expensive possessions are a responsibility.

"'Divine Mother,' I finally prayed, 'this coat is too good for me. Please take it away.'

"Soon afterwards I was scheduled to lecture at Trinity Auditorium. I sensed that the coat would be taken away from me that evening, so I emptied the pockets. After the lecture the coat was gone. What a relief!

"But then I spotted an omission. 'Divine Mother,' I prayed, 'You forgot to take the hat!'"

→2←

DURING THE LAST MONTHS of the Master's life, someone gave him an expensive Cadillac car. He referred to it several times as his "hangman's dinner."

"You know," he explained, "when someone is about to be executed by hanging, it is traditional to give him the best dinner possible. Divine Mother wanted, as a send-off, to give me something special because my work in this lifetime is finished."

→3←

YOUR HARD-EARNED MONEY, kept for safety in a bank, may be lost completely through the failure of that bank, but your well-controlled spiritual happiness, saved in the bank of your staunch, unchangeable determination, can never be lost, but will ever increase in value.

You are the officers, the president, and the directors, as well as the investors, in your own happiness-bank. If you know how to play these various roles, continually creating, preserving, and adding to your happiness deposits, then no failure can ever be possible for you, in your very own BANK OF HAPPINESS.

→ 4 ←

Portrait of a Businessman

THE BUSINESSMAN hurries to his office, rushes in, sits in his chair, and begins to concentrate upon some difficult problem. The din of his secretary's typewriter annoys him. He shouts at her to stop, but a moment later he realizes he needs the letter she is typing, so he shouts at her to continue typing. Then he begins smoking his after-breakfast cigar. Every day he resolves to quit smoking soon, as he knows it is a useless and expensive habit, but he never fulfills the resolution.

He tries to think more about the problem facing him, but ragged nerves tug at the sleeves of his concentration. Finally, he dashes the cigar into the ashtray, stops the typewriter, and dismisses his secretary when she brings him some bills that need to be paid.

He shouts at the outwardly respectful and inwardly laughing secretary, and pleads, "Have pity on me. Can't you see that I'm trying to put over a big deal?" As he tries to concentrate once more, unable to solve the problem, he dozes off. He then drifts into deeper slumber, while his secretary happily steals off to lunch. He wakes up to find that he has missed his train, missed his appointment, and that as a result, his big deal has fallen through. This businessman does not know the art of concentration.

The ordinary successful businessman uses only about twenty-five percent of his powers of concentration. But a student of these lessons can develop one hundred percent of his powers of concentration, and can use concentration to bring him success.

→5←

THE EGOTISTICAL MAN has plenty of time to speak to others of his greatness because he is not busy performing great deeds. But the great man is humble because he is so busy doing big things that he has no time to speak of his greatness.

The egotist, like an empty vessel, makes much noise, whereas the humble man is like a cask filled with the precious wine of wisdom.

→6←

Mistaken Identity

INTUITION MUST BE distinguished from self-confidence. Real intuition can never be wrong, but there are psychological states that pose as intuition and can bring trouble.

Once, on a farm, I met a man who had semi-developed intuition and bothered everybody with the display of his "intuition." He tried it on me several times, until I had an overdose of his semi-intuitional practices and decided to enlighten him.

One day, while we were sitting in his farm parlor, we heard a knock at the front door, so I asked my semi-intuitive friend, "Will you please tell me who is at the door?"

He immediately replied: "It is my uncle coming home after many years, and he never even wrote to tell me." The door was opened and the uncle appeared. When questioned, he said that he had come suddenly without notification.

My friend triumphantly exclaimed, "See, I have fully-developed intuition and not semi-developed intuition as you often say."

I remonstrated, "My friend, beware, or you will make a horrible blunder some time. You have had a little intuition all your life, but you have not practiced the technique to develop it to the point where you can totally depend upon it." He laughed at me, but soon I had the occasion to laugh at him. My mischievous prayer was answered.

One dismal, rainy day, as we sat in the farm parlor again, suddenly there was a loud knock on the closed door. I said to my friend, "Please use your semi-intuition and tell me who is knocking."

He concentrated for a moment, then said, "My brother has unexpectedly arrived. Open the door."

I laughed at him and replied, "No, not I. I wouldn't go near the door; my intuition tells me not to. You had better open the door yourself."

Saying this, I ran to the other side of the room. He opened the door, and in rushed the farm bull with menacing horns, angrily seeking shelter from the rain. My friend jumped aside frantically, and the bull ran after me. Of course, I was prepared for it and just stepped aside, loudly exclaiming, "My friend, your semi-intuition was indeed correct: your brother has arrived."

→ 7 ←
The Big Frog and the Little Frog

A BIG FAT FROG and a little frog fell into a milk pail with tall, slippery sides. They swam and swam for hours trying to get out. The big frog, exhausted, moaned, "Little brother frog, I am giving up!" and he sank to the bottom of the pail.

The little frog thought to himself, "If I give up I will die, so I must keep on swimming." Two hours passed, and the little frog thought he could do no more. But as he thought of his dead brother frog, he roused his will, saying, "To give up is certain death. I will keep on paddling until I die, if death is to come, but I will not give up trying, for while there is life there is still hope."

Intoxicated with determination, the little frog kept on paddling. After many hours, when he felt paralyzed with fatigue and could paddle no more, he suddenly felt a big lump under his feet. His incessant paddling had churned the milk into butter! Standing on the butter mound, with great joy the little frog leaped from the milk pail to freedom.

Remember, we are all in the slippery milk pail of life, like the two frogs, trying to get free from our troubles. Most people give up trying and fail, like the big frog. But we must learn to persevere in our effort toward one goal, as the little frog did. Then, we shall churn an opportunity by our God-guided, unflinching will power, and will be able to hop out of the milk pail of trials onto the safe ground of eternal success. By not giving up, we develop will power and win in everything we undertake.

→8←

The Magic Carrot

IN ANCIENT DAYS there lived in India a woman with a very quarrelsome disposition. She was named Kalaha, which means "quarrel" in Bengali. Miss Kalaha started word-battles with anyone at the slightest pretext, and she could brook no performance of any good action.

Time went by and Kalaha grew in her evil disposition and wickedness. At last, the Angel of Death cast her out of her body. Then her astral body began to descend the spiral stairway of gloom down into the deepest region of stygian darkness. She landed with a thud on the vapor-spitting floor of Hades. In agony and fright she shouted for mercy as she saw the Angel of Death leaving her in that dismal place, where sinful shadows live in torture and despair.

Somehow, attracted by the plaintive, intense noise of the wicked woman, Yama (the Angel of Death) returned and accosted her: "Please," he said, "can't you remember *any* good action which you performed during your earthly sojourn, so that I might parole you from this awful place you've landed because of your self-created errors?"

The wicked woman scratched her head for a while; after a long inner search, she cried out, "O yes, your Majesty, I do remember one kind act of mine. Once I had a bunch of carrots. I was about to eat them all when I found that one of them contained a worm, so I gave that wormy carrot to another person. I may even have suggested that he eat only the good part and throw away the rest without killing the worm."

"That will do," replied Yama. He waved his hand and that carrot came floating through the air toward the sin-filled woman. Yama continued, "Wicked soul, grasp this carrot and hang onto it. Don't loosen your hold, and it will take you up to Heaven."

The woman greedily seized the carrot and started her ascent heavenward. Seeing this, another sinner grasped her leg, and a second sinner grasped the leg of the first, and a third hung onto the legs of the second, until, gradually, a chain of one hundred sinners was suspended from the feet of the wicked woman. The magic carrot, with the wicked woman and the chain of one hundred sinners, began to rise toward Heaven like a zooming rocket.

The wicked woman was overjoyed to find herself so easily freed from the hands of after-death justice. Then she felt a tug at her feet, looked down, and realized that a long chain of sinners was going heavenward with her. The realization that they were all benefiting from this free ride infuriated her. She couldn't bear the thought of anyone else winning the favor of the Angel of Death. In rage she shouted, "You undeserving sinners, let go of my feet! How dare you soar toward Heaven with my charmed carrot?"

Kicking off the other sinners, she released her hold on the carrot. Thus, she and the whole chain plunged down through space, dropping with a thud on the floor of Hades.

The moral of the story is that even a small act of goodness may be a tiny raft of salvation across the treacherous gulf of sin, but one who drinks the wine of selfishness and dances on the little boat of meanness, sinks in the ocean of ignorance. Selfish happiness, which cannot bear to witness the well-being of others, is bound to come to grief.

Chapter 6

The Practice of Religion

→ 1 ←

"Sir," I asked Yogananda once, "what is faith? And how can one develop it?"

"Faith," was his answer, "comes with direct, personal experience. That is what Saint Paul meant when he said, 'Faith is the proof of things unseen.' The deeper your experience of truth, the greater the faith you will have.

"There was a man who had read in the Bible that if a person has sufficient faith, he will be able to say to this mountain, 'Be thou moved into the sea,' and it will be so. 'How wonderful!' the man thought. 'It has always bothered me that there is a mountain outside my window that obscures the view I might have, otherwise, of that beautiful lake on the other side. Let me remove the mountain by faith.'

"That night he prayed earnestly, 'Let the mountain be removed and cast into the sea.' He then went to bed. The next morning, the first thing he did was rush to the window to see what had happened. The mountain hadn't budged an inch.

"'I knew you'd still be there!' he cried.

"Such is the 'faith' of most people. Theirs isn't faith. It is merely belief."

→2←

THE MASTER LOVED TO relate this story: "Saint Teresa of Avila was crossing a stream with a few nuns. They were on their way to found a new convent. Teresa by this time was old and infirm.

"Suddenly the horse she was on was swept away in the stream, which was swollen by heavy rains. Her nuns were helpless to save her from drowning. They were sure she was lost.

"Teresa suddenly beheld Jesus Christ on the opposite bank. In no time, she found herself standing before him, completely dry.

"'Be of good cheer, Teresa!' Jesus said to her. 'This is how I treat all my friends.'

"Teresa answered joyfully, 'That, my Lord, is why You have so few!'

"That was a witty answer, but what a true one."

→3←

THE MASTER ONCE TOLD the story of a man who placed a hundred-dollar bill in the collection plate at church, then was upset because God didn't answer his prayer. Laughingly the

Master commented, "God already *was* that hundred-dollar bill—whether in or out of the collection plate! Why should He care where it was placed?"

↦4↤

SOMETIMES, WITH GREAT MERRIMENT, Yogananda paraphrased a story from the novel *Heavenly Discourse* by Charles E. Wood. His version of the tale went something like this: "When Billy Sunday, the famous evangelist, died and went to heaven, St. Peter wouldn't let him enter the Pearly Gates, demanding instead, 'What did you do on earth to deserve admission here?' 'Why,' Billy Sunday protested, 'what about all those thousands I sent up here from my revival meetings?' 'You may have sent them,' St. Peter retorted, 'but they never arrived!'"

↦5↤

The Miracle Man

A GREAT SAGE lived humbly with his wife, daughter, and a very spiritually inclined son. This sage kept his high spiritual attainments hidden from others behind a veneer of feigned worldliness. Some spiritual people, who deem God's love as their highest and most sacred possession, keep that love concealed from worldly eyes.

The son began to develop a craving for spirituality. In spite of his father's entreaties to stay home and find God there, the son left his family on a quest for a guru in the Himalayas. There he found a Tibetan miracle-man and remained under his tutelage for twenty years. The ascetic son became adept in performing wonders. Puffed up with the thought of his miraculous power, he returned to his native village. The little village hummed with excitement at the advent of this wonder-maker.

The miracle-filled son was full of braggadocio, and freely displayed his miraculous feats to the villagers. Exaggerated tales finally reached the ears of his humble, God-realized father. Curious, the father sent for his son. As father and son greeted each other, the son could not conceal his superiority complex. He began to brag about his miracles to his saintly father.

Humbly, the father inquired, "Son, what can you do?"

"What can I do?" sharply retorted the son with a smile of condescension on his lips. He led his holy father to the bank of the river Ganges and exclaimed, "Father, behold the wonder I can accomplish!"

The miracle-performing son quickly walked across the river Ganges to the far shore and back without even wetting his feet. "There, father, isn't that wonderful?" cried the son.

The father, who had been smiling hitherto, became grave, and gently admonished, "Son, for a long time I have been filled with happiness because I thought you had accomplished something real, but now I am very disappointed."

"How dare you ridicule my world-applauded miracles?" shouted the son.

Then the father explained, "My son, I see that you have wasted twenty precious years in learning a miraculous way to cross the Ganges, a feat which we accomplish simply by paying a ferryman four cents. Pray tell me, why did you throw away twenty years just to save four cents?"

The son awoke from his dream of pride and stood with bowed head before the wisdom of his father, who continued, "Son, to love miracles more than the Fountain of all powers, God, *is error*. To love false, evanescent power in lieu of permanent, unending power is folly. To love short-lasting miracles in preference to the everlasting miracle of God-contact, is foolishness."

So saying, the father fell silent and the son bowed before him.

→ 6 ←

The Bad Man Who Was Preferred by God

GOD SENT HIS ARCHANGEL Narada on a heavenly errand to find His true devotees on earth. Garbed as a saintly human being, Narada had just started on his earthly journey when he came upon a hoary anchorite practicing several different postures and penances under a tamarind tree. Saint Narada approached the old man and said, "Hello, who are you, and what are you doing?"

The man replied, "Honored Sir, my name is Bhadraka. I am an anchorite who has been practicing rigorous physical discipline for eighty years."

Narada replied, "Well, I came from Heaven to find a true devotee of God."

The anchorite laughingly remarked, "Honored one, your eyes are now beholding the greatest devotee of God on earth. Rain or shine, for eighty years I have practiced every imaginable technique of mental and physical self-torturing discipline for attaining knowledge."

Narada said, "Revered anchorite, I am very touched by your devotion."

"Well, then," hoarsely bellowed the anchorite Bhadraka, "when next you meet God, please ask him why He has kept away from me for so long."

Saint Narada happily agreed and continued on his journey.

At one point he paused to watch an amusing incident by the roadside. There stood a young man, totally drunk, trying to build a fence, and vainly attempting to put a bamboo fence post into a small hole. In utter frustration, he was loudly cursing and shouting, "You naughty God, if You don't come help me get this pole into the hole, I'm going to thrust the bamboo into Your heart."

The young man, in his intoxicated fog, suddenly noticed the staring Saint Narada and shouted, "Hey, you good-for-nothing idler, how dare you look at me like that?"

Saint Narada, taken aback, replied, "May I help you to set your bamboo pole?"

To this the drunken young man promptly replied, "No sir, I will accept help from no one but that Sly Eluder, God, who has been playing hide-and-seek with me, trying to get out of helping me."

Narada, with mild derision said, "You drunken fool, aren't you afraid to curse God?"

"Not at all, He understands me better than you do," was the instantaneous reply. "Who are you?" the young man demanded.

"I am an angel from Heaven, and I've come to find the true devotees of God on earth."

"Oh, is that what you are here for? Well, please put in a good word for me to God, even though I have been somewhat bad, and ask Him when He is coming to visit me?"

Reluctantly, Narada agreed to the request, but inwardly thought, "You have a fat chance of seeing God!"

Disgusted with this scene, Narada left for Heaven. With great enthusiasm he knelt before his Heavenly Majesty. The Heavenly King gently demanded, "Dear Narada, tell me all about your earthly excursions."

"Well, my King," said Narada, "sometimes I wonder if You are too hard to please. Do You know about that anchorite Bhadraka, under the tamarind tree?"

God scratched His hoary head and replied, "No, I don't remember him."

"Beloved God, how is that possible? That man has been practicing all sorts of discipline for eighty years to please You," replied Narada.

But God insisted, "No matter what the anchorite has been doing, he has never touched My heart. Anyone else?" God asked.

With reluctance, Narada said, "I met—" but before he could finish, God interrupted him and finished the sentence by saying: "You met a drunken young man."

"I am totally surprised that you remember this man, your Heavenly Majesty. Perhaps because he has been poking You with bamboo poles."

God laughed heartily and lovingly said: "O my Narada, don't get angry with me, nor be sarcastic, for I will prove to you which of the two men you saw on earth is a true devotee.

"Narada, visit earth again and go to the anchorite Bhadraka and say, 'I gave your message to God, but He is very busy now passing a million elephants through the eye of a needle. When He finishes, He will visit you.' After you hear the anchorite's response, tell the same thing to the drunken young man and watch his reaction. Then you will understand."

When Narada brought God's message to the old anchorite, Bhadraka flew into a rage and shouted, "Get out, you and God and all your crazy crowd! Who ever heard of anyone passing elephants through the eye of a needle? These eighty years of discipline are nothing but folly. I am through trying to please a crazy, nonexistent God. I am going to become sane and enjoy what fun I can in my remaining years."

Taken aback by these astonishing remarks, Narada quickly left to visit the young man, whom he found drunker than ever, cursing more than ever, and trying to fix another bamboo pole for the fence. But no sooner had Narada appeared on the scene than the young man's intoxication seemed to leave him; in its place was the intoxication of joy. He came running, and cried, "Saint Narada, what did God say in answer to my question?"

When the young man heard God's message, he began to dance round and round with joy, saying, "He who can send worlds through the eye of a needle in an instant if He desires, has already finished passing elephants through the eye of a needle. Any moment now He will be with me. When He comes, my love for Him will make me forget my drinking habit and all my evil actions."

As the young man danced in heavenly ecstasy, Narada joined him, and soon they found that God was dancing in their midst.

This story illustrates that no matter how many years you have been going to church or doing good works, unless you love God, He will never reveal Himself to you.

And, even if you have not been able to give up bad habits despite your efforts, if you have supremely intoxicated yourself with the love of God, He will reveal Himself to you. With the dawning of His presence, the darkness of evil habits will vanish from your soul.

CHAPTER 7

CONCENTRATION AND MEDITATION

→1←

Just as you could not hope to meditate with the noise of a vacuum cleaner going on near you, so you cannot meditate deeply while beset with the noises of the heart and lungs, as they surge and swirl in your physical body to clear away the "dirt" of venous blood, until you have stilled them by watching the breath.

→2←

A popular but ineffectual method of concentration may be depicted by this useless attempt. The scene is an apartment, about 2 p.m. on a wintry day.

A lady enters, pulls down the shades, and hurries to sit in a straight-backed chair to concentrate. No sooner has her body touched the chair than she exclaims, "My goodness, this seat is too hard. Let me fetch a pillow." Seated on the pillow, she suddenly discovers that the chair is maliciously squeaking and disturbing the beginnings of her concentration. So she transfers her pillow and her body to another chair.

"Now, at last, everything is right for a delightful dip into the depths of concentration." Only a moment passes and she is about to plunge within, when, "*Ta, ta, ta, ta, tang, ta, ta, tang*" sings the boiling radiator. In disgust, she chokes the radiator's voice. In righteous indignation she now increases her determination to dive deep into the heart of meditation.

A moment later, "*Plung, ploong, ploong-plung*" goes the piano in the apartment next door. Annoyed, she thinks, "There goes that terrible piano again, just as I sit down to meditate."

As her wrath calms down in the semi-darkness, she begins to think, "Well, that's really a fairly good piano; it only needs a little tuning." Then comes the memory of her dear grandmother's piano in the sweet old days of long ago—her dear grandmother, who always protected her from the harsh discipline of her parents . . . followed by more loving thoughts of her grandmother.

Suddenly, she jerks herself from her reverie and remembers, "Oh, I must practice silence; I must concentrate." So, with saintly dignity, her spirit rebuked for its restlessness, with rather battered self-control, she once more attempts to meditate.

Her eyes have hardly closed again when "*Br Br Brr Brrrrrrring—*" crows the telephone with impudent, patience-piercing pertinacity. She breathes to herself through grinding teeth, "I will not answer. Crow all you like, Mr. Telephone." But *"Brrrrrrring"* goes the impertinent bell with unimaginable persistency.

"Well, maybe it is an important call. 'Hello, there—What is it you want? This is Somerville 2924. . . .'" As she hears the soul-exasperating answer, "Wrong number," she slams the mouthpiece onto the hook.

This terrible ordeal over, she musters enough courage to again try to concentrate, while her brain seethes with the thought, "I will break that telephone forever. It will then disturb me no more." With scissors in hand, she is about to cut the cord when she thinks of the inconvenience that might follow, so she changes her mind and puts a piece of cardboard between the hammer and the bell on the telephone.

That accomplished, victorious, she sits once more on her throne of concentration. A few more minutes pass and she is half-dozing because of her battles with piano noises, the telephone, and so forth. Catching herself sleeping, half-ashamed, she sits up straight once more to begin again to meditate. Immediately there arises a clamorous ringing of her doorbell. As before, she thinks, "I will not answer it."

The doorbell goes on ringing until she thinks again, "Maybe it is something important." At the door she assumes a galvanized smile as she greets her three lady friends, who have all obtained a master's degree in the art of gossiping, and she gushes, "How do you do? Come right in, you three darlings. I'm so delighted that you've come over." Behind the forced smile lies the silent whispering, "Oh, you pests and gossips, when will you go so that I can concentrate?"

Three hours slip away as she merrily laughs at the folly of her three gossiping cronies. At last, the door closes behind their vanishing forms. Much relieved, the lady once more sits down to seek her lost throne of silence, but her attention is mobbed by memories of radiators, piano noises, telephone bells, door bells, and gossips. She looks at her watch and says, with a resigned sigh, "I give up, dear Concentration. It seems that I cannot be with you today. I have to run now to prepare the evening meal."

The above experience is only a sample of what happens to most women and men when they attempt to concentrate. God tries to speak to His children through the voice of silence and peace in response to their prayers, but His voice is usually drowned out by the ringing of telephones, sensations of touch, smell, taste, hearing, and sight, and by the rowdy noises of their sensation- and memory-roused thoughts. Sadly, God turns away.

→3←
"Monkey Consciousness"

TEJ BAHADUR, a successful young businessman in India, spent considerable amounts of money to travel to London for his business transactions. Extremely economical, he was always looking for new ways to save money.

A friend of his, who knew about his desire to economize, came scurrying toward him with a volley of excited words: "Tej Bahadur, come to the banks of the river Ganges," he said. "I have found a man who can levitate and walk on water, and who is willing to teach the method to a worthy student."

Tej Bahadur was greatly impressed with this new idea and said to himself, "Thank God for sending me a levitating tutor. I will ask him to teach me levitation, and that will save me a lot of money on my European business trips."

And so he went to the riverbank and asked the master to teach him to levitate. The master agreed and immediately began his lesson: "Son, every night, lock the doors in your bedroom, dim the light, and sit erect on a straight-backed chair facing east. With closed eyes, mentally chant the holy sound of AUM for an hour. At the end of one month, you will be able to race over the waters."

The businessman thanked the master for the lesson and was about to return home, when the master called him back and cautioned him gently: "Son, I forgot to tell you one thing. While you are mentally chanting AUM, be sure not to think of monkeys." "That is simple," said the businessman, "Of course I won't think of monkeys." After saluting the saint, he returned home.

As evening came Tej Bahadur closed the windows, pulled down the shades, and sat in a straight chair to practice the technique from the master. The first thought that struck him like a thunderbolt was, "I must not think of monkeys."

Two minutes passed and several times he warned himself inwardly, "I must not think of monkeys." When ten minutes had passed, he had thought of all the different kinds of monkeys in South America, India, Africa, and Sumatra. He was furious. He willed himself to banish thoughts of monkeys, which were leaping through the window of his helpless mind. At the end of an hour he found himself thinking of nothing but monkeys. With each succeeding day he meditated faithfully, but to his great annoyance he found that he was always frantically trying not to think of the millions of monkeys jumping into his mind.

After a month's concentration upon the forbidden monkeys, the businessman, beside himself with helpless fury, raced back to the master and exclaimed loudly, "Master, take back your lesson on levitation. I don't want to learn to walk on the water. You have taught me to meditate upon monkeys, instead of how to levitate. You have developed the monkey consciousness in me."

"Ha, ha, ha," laughed the saint merrily, then spoke to him soothingly: "Son, I needed to show you how untrained is your state of concentration. Until you learn to make your mind obey you, you cannot achieve any success, what to speak of attaining the power of levitation. First learn to attain mental control, then use that power to achieve small things. When you are able to do that, try bigger and bigger achievements, until your inner power becomes developed enough to levitate you, or to accomplish even greater spiritual miracles."

→ 4 ←

The Man Who Became a Buffalo

ON THE SIDE OF A MOUNTAIN was a cozy hermitage where dwelt a great master with a devoted disciple. Daily, the master would ask his disciple to sit upright in a perfect meditating posture and listen to his teachings with absorbed attention.

One day the master noticed that his young disciple was absent-minded and restless, so he gently said to him, "Son, your mind is not on my words. Pray tell me, what is the reason for your absent-mindedness?"

The disciple respectfully replied, "Honored Master, I cannot concentrate on your lesson today, for my mind is helplessly thinking about my newly acquired tame buffalo, which is grazing on the green plants of the valley."

The guru, instead of scolding the disciple, calmly asked him to retire into a small room, close the door, and think of nothing but the buffalo. One day passed, and the next morning the master looked in on his disciple and asked, "Son, what are you doing?"

"Sir, I am watching the buffalo graze in the field. Shall I come out now?"

"No, Son, not yet; go on enjoying your buffalo."

Another day passed and, on the third morning, the master again looked in on him and asked, "Beloved Child, what are you doing?" To which the disciple, in a state of ecstasy, replied, "Heavenly Master, I behold the buffalo in my room, and I am feeding it. Shall I come to you with my buffalo?"

"Not yet, my son. Go on with the vision of feeding the buffalo."

Another two days passed in meditation on the buffalo. On the fifth day, once again the guru spoke to the disciple: "Son, pray tell me, what are you doing now?"

The disciple answered in a deep, bellowing voice, "What do you mean? I am not your son. I am a buffalo."

To this, the master smilingly replied, "All right, Mr. Buffalo, you can come out now."

"How can I get out through that narrow door?" the disciple rumbled. "My body is too large and my horns are too wide." Then the master went into the small room, touched the "buffalo," and brought him out of his trance. The disciple smiled to find himself walking on all fours, imitating the object of his meditation.

Then the disciple went to listen to the words of his master. The master asked him many deep, spiritual questions, all of which the disciple answered correctly, as never before. At last the guru remarked, "Now your concentration has reached the perfect state; you and your mind can be one with the object of study."

→5←

The Lion Who Became a Sheep

A LIONESS, huge with an unborn baby lion, was growing weak from lack of food. As her baby grew heavier within her, she could no longer move quickly enough to catch any prey.

Roaring with sadness and hunger, and heavy with the baby lion, the lioness fell asleep at the edge of the forest near a pasture. As she dozed, she dreamt of seeing a flock of sheep grazing. When, in her dream, she pounced on one of the sheep, she jerked herself awake. With surprise and great joy she discovered that her dream was true: a large flock of sheep grazed in the pasture right near her.

Forgetting the heavy unborn cub in her body, and impelled by the madness of hunger, the lioness pounced on one of the young lambs and carried it into the depths of the forest. The lioness did not realize that during the exertion of her mad leap at the lamb she had given birth to a baby lion.

The flock of sheep were so paralyzed with fear by the attack of the lioness that they couldn't run away. When the lioness had departed and the panic was over, the sheep woke from their stupor. They were beginning to bleat out lamentations for their lost comrade when, to their great astonishment, they discovered the helpless baby lion crooning in their midst. One of the mother sheep took pity on the baby lion and adopted it as her own.

The young lion grew up amidst the flock of sheep. Years passed, and there, with a flock of sheep, roamed a huge lion with long mane and tail, behaving exactly like a sheep. The sheep-lion bleated instead of roaring and ate grass instead of meat. This vegetarian lion acted exactly like a weak, meek lamb.

One day another lion strolled out of the nearby forest onto the green pasture, and to his great delight beheld this flock of sheep. Thrilled with joy and whipped by hunger, the great lion was pursuing the fleeing sheep when, with amazement, he spied a huge lion, with tail high up in the air, racing at top speed ahead of the flock.

The older lion paused for a moment, scratched his head, and pondered, "I can understand the sheep flying away from me, but I cannot imagine why this stalwart lion should run at the sight of me. This runaway lion interests me." Ignoring his hunger, he ran hard and pounced upon the escaping lion. The sheep-lion fainted with fear. The big lion was puzzled more than ever, and slapped the sheep-lion out of his swoon.

In a deep voice he rebuked, "What's the matter with you?! Why do you, my brother, flee from me?"

The sheep-lion closed his eyes and bleated out in sheep language, "Please let me go. Don't kill me. I'm just a sheep brought up with yonder flock."

"Oh, now I see why you're bleating." The big lion pondered again, and a great idea flashed upon him. He caught the sheep-lion by the mane with his mighty jaws and dragged him toward a lake at the end of the pasture. When the big lion reached the shore of the lake, he pushed the sheep-lion's head so that it was reflected in the water. He began to shake the sheep-lion, who still had his eyes tightly closed, saying, "Open your eyes! Look! You are not a sheep."

"*Bleat, bleat, bleat.* Please don't kill me. Let me go. I am only a poor, meek sheep," wailed the sheep-lion.

The big lion gave the sheep-lion a terrible shake. The sheep-lion opened his eyes, and was astonished to find the reflection of his head was not a sheep's head as he expected, but a lion's head, like that of the one who was shaking him with his paw. Then the big lion said, "Look at my face and your face reflected in the water. They are the same. My face roars. Now! You must roar instead of bleating."

The sheep-lion, convinced, tried to roar, but could only produce tepid cries, mingled with bleats. As the older lion continued to exhort him with slapping paws, the sheep-lion at last succeeded in roaring. Then both of the lions bounded across the pasture, and returned to live in the den of lions.

The above story aptly illustrates how most of us, though made in the image of the all-powerful Divine Lion of the Universe, have been born and brought up in the sheepfold of mortal weakness. We bleat with fear, lack, and death, instead of roaring with immortality and power.

These spiritual teachings are the new lion that will drag you to the crystal pool of meditation and give you such a hard shaking that you will open the closed eyes of your wisdom and behold yourself as a Lion of Divinity, made in the image of the Cosmic Lion. Those of you who strive continuously will forget your mortal fears of weakness, failure, and death, and will learn to roar with the power of almighty immortality.

Chapter *8*

STORIES FROM HIS EARLY YEARS

→ 1 ←

"When I first started on my own in the spiritual life, I settled in a little mud hut with two other boys. One of them was about my size: short and slight. The other was a big, stalwart fellow. One day I said to them, 'Let's lay a cement floor in the main room.'

"'Impossible!' protested the big fellow. 'We don't have the cement; we don't have the equipment; we don't have the know-how; we don't have the money. For a technical job like this you need experience.'

"'If we make up our minds,' I replied, 'we can do it.'

"'Wishful thinking!' he scoffed, and walked away to show what he thought of the scheme.

"That day the other boy and I went around to the neighbors. Bit by bit we gathered donations of materials, and loans of equipment. Two men added careful instructions on how to mix and lay the cement. That whole night we stayed up, mixing and pouring. By the following morning the job was finished. The big fellow returned later to our little hermitage.

"'Well,' I sighed, teasing him, 'I guess you were right.'

"'Aha,' he cried. 'You see? I told you so!'

"I then asked him please to fetch me something from the next room. He opened the door. And there was our new cement floor! We'd even colored it red. He was dumbfounded."

→2←

"Once as a boy, during meditation, I entered a state of ecstasy. My breathing and heartbeat were stilled. Then I decided to play a little prank. Well, after all, I was only a boy! When people came in they saw me lying there, apparently lifeless. What a commotion! What wails! What lamentation! All the family stood around saying how highly they'd thought of me.

"And then an old, faithful servant of the family, whom we used to call Maid Ma, cried loudly, 'Ah! Ah! Now I won't have anyone to fight with anymore!' That was too much for me! I couldn't contain myself any longer.

"'Oh yes, you will!' I cried.

"'You!' she shouted angrily. 'I knew you were only fooling!' She picked up a broom and flung it at me.

"Was it naughty of me? Well, I must say, it was great fun!"

→3←

"I used to wear a beard. On the ship coming over from India, a fellow passenger, a Muslim by the name of Rashid, persuaded me to shave it off. Americans, he insisted, might accept me if I had *either* long hair *or* a beard, but definitely not if I kept both. Since my master had expressed a wish that I keep my hair long, I decided to sacrifice the beard. Rashid volunteered his services as a barber. I placed myself trustingly in his hands. He lathered my face, then proceeded carefully to shave off one half of it. At that point, he walked off, abandoning me! And I had no notion of how to shave! I was stranded until, after some hours, he returned, laughing, to complete the job.

"Rashid was a great prankster. But he was also very helpful to me when I began my first lecture tour. He got the halls, prepared the publicity, and acted as my secretary. Still, he did play pranks!

"One evening, however, I got the better of him. He was always avoiding his work, and running after girls. He didn't realize that I knew what he was doing. On this particular evening he'd promised to come in and work with me. When he didn't show up, I knew just where to find him. I went to a nearby park, and there he was, sitting on a bench with a new girl. (He certainly had a way with them!) I crept up stealthily from behind and stood nearby, hidden by a bush. He put his arms around the girl, and was just about to kiss her, when I cried out in a deep, loud voice, 'Rasheeeed!' You should have seen him jump! He came regularly into the office after that, and worked quite docilely!"

We all laughed uproariously at Master's story, which was delivered with suitably droll gestures and expressions.

→4←

"BECAUSE OF MY ROBE and long hair, people sometimes thought I was a woman. Once, at a Boston flower exhibition, I wanted to find the men's room. A guard directed me to a certain door. Trustingly I went in. My goodness! Ladies to the left of me, ladies to the right of me, ladies everywhere! I rushed out, and once more approached the guard.

"'I want the *men's* room,' I insisted. Eyeing me suspiciously, he finally pointed to another door. This time as I entered a man cried out, 'Not in here, lady! Not in here!'

"In a deep bass voice I answered, 'I know what I am doing!'

"Another time on a train the black conductor kept walking up and down the aisle, eyeing me. Finally he could restrain his curiosity no longer. 'Is yo' a man,' he asked, 'or is yo' a woman?'

"'What do you theenk?' I demanded in a deep, booming tone."

→5←

You don't have to *own* a thing to enjoy it," Master told us. "To possess things is all right, provided your possessions don't possess you, but ownership often means only added worries. It is much better to own everything in God, and cling to nothing with your ego."

Smiling, he continued, "Years ago I visited Radio City Music Hall in New York. Having paid the price of admission, I told myself, 'While I am here, this building is mine!' I walked about, enjoying my beautiful acquisition. When I had enjoyed it as much as I cared to, I gave the building back to the management with thanks, and walked out a free man!"

6

"One evening in Chicago I visited a park. It was during the Depression years, and Chicago, as you know, was notorious at the time for its gangsters. A policeman stopped me as I was about to enter the park, and warned me that it wasn't safe there after dark. 'Even we are afraid to go in,' he said.

"Well, I went in anyway, and took a seat comfortably on a park bench. After some time, a tough-looking man, much larger than I, stopped in front of me.

"'Gimme a dime!' he snarled.

"I reached into a pocket and gave him a dime.

"'Gimme a quarter!' I gave him a quarter.

"'Gimme fifty cents.' I gave him fifty cents.

"'Gimme a dollar.'

"By now, seeing that matters obviously weren't going to improve, I leapt to my feet and, with God's power, shouted:

"'GET OUT!!!'

"The man began to tremble like a leaf. 'I don't want your money!' he mumbled. Backing fearfully away, he repeated, 'I don't want your money! I don't want your money!' Suddenly he turned and fled as though his life depended on it.

"I sat down peacefully once more and watched the moonrise. Later, as I was leaving the park, the same policeman as before saw me and asked, 'What did you say to that man? I saw him with you, and didn't dare to interfere. I know him for a dangerous character!'

"'Oh,' I replied, 'we came to a little understanding.'"

→7←

MANY WERE SURPRISED to learn how physically powerful Master was. He was quite short—five feet five or six inches—and, though well built, didn't impress one as being particularly strong. But his strength came primarily from his complete command over the energy in his body.

"In Symphony Hall in Boston," he told us, "I was lecturing once on the merits of the energization exercises, and mentioned the great physical strength one derives from them. I then threw out the challenge: 'Would anyone here like to *try* my strength?'

"Six tall, burly policemen jumped up onto the stage! The audience gasped, certain that I'd fail this test.

"Well, facing them, I placed my back against the wall. Then I asked the men to push on my stomach all together, as hard as they could. They did so. 'Is that the best you can do?' I demanded.

"'Yeah!' they grunted, clenching their teeth.

"Suddenly I arched my back. All six of them went tumbling back into the orchestra pit!"

→8←

"I used sometimes to go to movies," Master told us, "to get away from the unceasing demands of the work. Sitting in the movie theater, I would enter samadhi. Later, if people asked me how I liked the movie, I replied, 'Very much!' I had been watching the cosmic 'movie,' with stars and planets whirling through space!"

No environment was wholly mundane to him. Everywhere he saw God. "Do you know where I wrote my poem 'Samadhi'?" he asked us one day. "It was on the New York subway! As I was writing, I rode back and forth from one end of the line to the other. No one asked for my ticket. In fact," he added with a twinkle in his eyes, "no one even saw me!"

Chapter 9

Training the Disciples

→1←

BERNARD WAS A MONASTIC DISCIPLE and a minister of Self-Realization Fellowship who conducted services in the SRF Church in Hollywood. Certain women in the congregation had been saying they thought he would look well in a turban. The Master made no comment on the point. He determined, however, to quiet this little ripple of interest before it grew to become a wave.

A formal Indian gathering had been scheduled. For the event, the Master dressed Bernard in a turban. He wound a long strip of cloth with great care around the disciple's head—arranging it in such a way, however, that although the turban managed to stay on, it would slip lopsidedly over one eye, then over the other eye, and manage always to look ridiculous.

Did Bernard enjoy the comedy? . . . He was the sort of person who might well have responded, with Queen Victoria, "We are not amused." It was an elderly nun who, gleefully but not unkindly, told me the story.

→2←

ONE TIME, WHILE TRAVELING BY CAR with a group of nuns, the Master made them stop by the roadside on a main highway, get out, and consume a large, very juicy watermelon. He cut it into unwieldy pieces which made sure the juice got all over their arms, hands, and faces: not the sort of spectacle that women—especially young ones—like to present for public inspection. The Master was unconcerned for their embarrassment. They too, after their initial shock, accepted the situation with good humor.

→3←

LIKE MOST COLLEGE-TRAINED INTELLECTUALS, my notion of wisdom tended to be rather dry. But until the intellect has been softened by heart qualities, it is like earth without water: weighty but infertile. Master was anxious to wean me from this addiction to an arid mental diet, even as I myself was anxious to be weaned.

One evening Norman and I were sitting with him in the kitchen. Master summoned one of the sisters and asked her to fetch a brown paper bag with something in it from his bedroom. When she returned, he switched off the lights. I heard him remove something from the bag, then chuckle playfully. Suddenly there was a metallic buzzing sound as sparks came leaping out of a toy pistol. Laughing with childlike glee, Master turned the lights back on. Next, from another toy pistol out of the bag, he shot a tiny parachute into the air. We watched together gravely as it descended to the floor. I was utterly astonished.

Master glanced at me merrily, though with a covert gaze of calm understanding. 'How do you like them, Walter?'

I laughed, trying earnestly to enter into the spirit of the occasion. 'They're fine, Sir!' My comment was almost an affirmation.

Looking at me deeply now, but with love, he quoted the words of Jesus: 'Suffer little children to come unto me, for of such is the kingdom of God.'

→ 4 ←

EARLY ONE RATHER MILD AUTUMN EVENING he was seated in his car, chatting with a few of us before going out for a drive. He was explaining some philosophical point, when, midway through his explanation, he paused and inquired, "Isn't it rather hot today?"

We hesitated, knowing that he had it in mind to give us money for ice cream. He looked at us expectantly. At last I said, smiling, "Well, it *was* hot, Sir, but by now it has cooled off."

"Too bad!" Master laughed playfully. "You've cheated yourselves out of some refreshments!" He returned to his discourse. Several more minutes passed, then he paused again.

"You're *sure* it isn't a bit warm this evening?"

"Well," we replied laughing, "it is if you say so, Sir!"

Decisively he concluded, "I can't keep money and I won't! Here, take these dollars for ice cream. I like having money only so that I can give it away."

→5←

TO ONE OF THE YOUNGER RENUNCIATES he said one day, "You have devotion, but you are always joking and keeping the others rollicking. You must learn to be more serious."

"I know it, Sir," the young man replied sadly, "but my habit is strong. How can I change without your blessing?"

"Well, *my* blessing is there already. *God's* blessing is there. Only *your* blessing is lacking!"

→6←

DR. LEWIS and several other disciples, including Mrs. Lewis and Norman, accompanied the Master to San Francisco to meet Jawaharlal Nehru, India's Prime Minister. Doctor returned to Mt. Washington with tales of their journey.

"Master," Doctor reported, "asked me to join him one morning in practicing the energization exercises on the hotel porch in San Francisco." Doctor chuckled. "I nearly died of embarrassment! But what good reason can there be, after all, to feel embarrassed about doing a good thing? My self-consciousness had no worthier basis than the fact that our exercises aren't known to most people! Master decided to cure me of this false notion.

"As we were exercising, a policeman walked by on his beat. Master, affecting a guilty conscience, stepped hastily behind a pillar, continuing to exercise there. The policeman glanced at us suspiciously. I was praying for a miracle that would dematerialize me on the spot! But Master went right on exercising as though nothing had happened.

"Minutes later, the policeman returned. Again Master ducked behind the pillar. This time the man, his suspicions thoroughly aroused, came over to us.

"'What's going on here?' he demanded. He probably suspected us of being a pair of crooks planning a crime.

"'Oh, *nothing*, Officer!' Master assured him with an exaggerated air of innocence. 'Nothing at all. We're just exercising. See?' To demonstrate his utter sincerity, he repeated a few movements, then smiled as if in hopeful expectation of a reprieve.

"'Well,' muttered the officer, 'see that you don't get into trouble.' With massive dignity he moved on. By this time I was shaking so hard with suppressed mirth that my embarrassment was completely forgotten."

→7←

DURING THE TRIP to San Francisco, Master and the Lewises had adjoining hotel rooms. "Master kept the door open between us," Doctor said. "I knew he didn't really want us to sleep that night. He himself never sleeps, you know. Not, at least, in the way you and I do; he's always in superconsciousness. And he wants to break *us*, too, of too much dependence on subconsciousness—'counterfeit samadhi,' he calls it. So I guess he saw here an opportunity for us to spend a few hours in sharing spiritual friendship and inspiration with him. We don't get many chances for that any more, now that the work has become worldwide.

"The problem was, Mrs. Lewis and I were both tired—she especially so. We'd been traveling all day. 'We're going to sleep,' she announced in a tone of finality. That, as far as she was concerned, was that.

"Master, however, had other ideas.

"Mrs. Lewis and I went to bed. Master, apparently submissive, lay down on his bed. I was just getting relaxed, and Mrs. Lewis was beginning to drift peacefully off to sleep, when all at once Master, as though with deep relevance, said:

"'Sub gum.'

"Nothing more. Sub gum was the name of one of those Chinese dishes we'd eaten earlier that day. I smiled to myself. But Mrs. Lewis muttered with grim earnestness, 'He's *not* going to make me get up!' A few minutes passed. We were just drifting off again, when suddenly, in marveling tones:

"'Sub gum *duff*!' Master pronounced the words carefully, like a child playing with unaccustomed sounds.

"Desperately Mrs. Lewis whispered, 'We're sleeping!' She turned for help to the wall.

"More minutes passed. Then, very slowly:

"'*Super* sub gum duff!' The words this time were spoken earnestly, like a child making some important discovery.

"By this time I was chuckling to myself. But though sleep was beginning to seem rather an 'impossible dream' for both of us, Mrs. Lewis was still hanging on fervently to her resolution.

"More minutes passed. And then the great discovery:

"'Super SUBMARINE sub gum duff!'

"Further resistance was impossible! Howling with merriment, we rose from the bed. For the remainder of the night, sleep was forgotten. We talked and laughed with Master. Gradually the conversation shifted to serious matters. We ended up speaking of spiritual matters, then meditating. With his blessings, we felt no further need for sleep that night.

→8←

"I was telling you," Dr. Lewis continued, "that Master never sleeps. I've found this to be true even when he snores! One day, many years ago, he was lying in his room, apparently asleep, and snoring quite loudly. I tiptoed stealthily into the room and tied a string to his big toe, doing my best to make sure he felt nothing. I should add that we were both young then. Master was still snoring peacefully as I crept back to the door. I was about to tie the string onto the doorknob when he stopped snoring long enough to say, 'Aha!'"

→9←

"MASTER ONCE TAUGHT ME a good lesson on the attitude we should hold toward our work." Mrs. Vera Brown (later, Meera Mata), an advanced older disciple whom Master had made responsible for training some of the newer ones, was sharing with me a few of her experiences with our Guru.

"'You work too hard,' Master told me one day. 'You *must* work less. If you don't, you will ruin your health.'

"'Very well,' I thought, 'I'll try not doing so much.'

"Two or three days later, to my surprise, Master gave me *more* work to do!"

Mrs. Brown's eyes twinkled. "'Okay, Master,' I thought, 'you must know what you're doing.' I took on my new duties. But all the time I kept wondering, 'How am I going to reconcile all this extra work with his instructions to me to work *less*?'

"Well, a couple of days after that, Master again told me, more sternly this time, 'You *must not* work so hard. In this lifetime you've done enough work for several incarnations.'

"What was I to do? Again I tried cutting down my activities, only to find Master, after two or three days, giving me more work than ever!

"We repeated this little comedy several times. Every time Master told me to work *less*, he added duties soon thereafter that forced me to work *more*. I figured he must know what he was doing, and that it was up to me to try and understand what that was.

"Well, finally one day I looked at Master. 'Sir,' I said, 'instead of using the word *work* in our life here, why don't we substitute the word *service*?'

"Master laughed. 'It has been a good show,' he said. 'All your life you've been thinking, *work! work! work!* That very thought was exhausting you. But just see how differently you feel when you think of work as a divine service! When you act to please God, you can do *twice* as much and never feel tired!'"

→10←

Mrs. Brown laughed merrily. "Master also taught me a good lesson on the subject of maintaining the consciousness of God's presence.

"He was cooking one day in his kitchen. I was there in the room with him. For lack of anything better to do, I decided I'd clean up after him. The moment he emptied one pan, I'd wash it. Whenever he spilled anything, I cleaned up the mess.

"Well, he began dirtying pans and more pans, spilling food and more food. I was working faster and faster to keep up with him. In my whole life I'd *never* seen such sloppy cooking! At last I just gave up. It occurred to me that I might as well wait till he was finished before I did any more.

"As I sat down to watch him, I noticed a little smile on his face, though he said nothing. Presently, I saw he wasn't messing things up any more. Finally it dawned on me that he'd only been teaching me the difference between calm, God-reminding activity, and the sort of restlessness that one indulges in just for activity's sake. I'd been working in a spirit of busy-ness. Master's way of showing me my mistake was to lead me to its own logical conclusion!"

Chapter *10*

Stories with a Moral

→1←

Reincarnation in a Nutshell

THERE WAS A MAN who loved God and had achieved a little spiritual advancement, but who also had a few worldly desires left to fulfill. At the end of his life an angel appeared to him and asked, "Is there anything you still want?"

"Yes," the man said, "All my life I've been weak, thin, and unwell. I would like in my next life to have a strong, healthy body."

In his next life he was given a strong, large, and healthy body. He was poor, however, and found it difficult to keep that robust body properly fed. At last—still hungry—he lay dying. The angel appeared to him again and asked, "Is there anything more you desire?"

"Yes," he replied. "For my next life, I would like a strong, healthy body, and also a healthy bank account!"

Well, the next time he had a strong, healthy body, and was also wealthy. In time, however, he began to grieve that he had no one with whom to share his good fortune. When death came, the angel asked, "Is there anything else?"

"Yes, please. Next time, I would like to be strong, healthy, and wealthy, and also to have a good woman for a wife."

Well, in his next life he was given all those blessings. His wife, too, was a good woman. Unfortunately, she died in her youth. For the rest of his days, he grieved at that loss. He worshiped her gloves, her shoes, and other memorabilia that were precious to him. As he lay dying of grief, the angel appeared to him again and said, "What now?"

"Next time," said the man, "I would like to be strong, healthy, and wealthy, and also to have a good wife who lives a long time."

"Are you sure you've covered everything?" demanded the angel.

"Yes, I'm certain that's everything this time."

Well, in his next life he had all those things, including a good wife who lived a long time. The trouble was, she lived too long! As he grew older, he became infatuated with his beautiful young secretary, to the point where, finally, he left his good wife for that girl. As for the girl, all she wanted was his money. When she'd got her hands on it, she ran away with a much younger man. At last, as the man lay dying, the angel again appeared to him and demanded. "Well, what is it this time?"

"Nothing!" the man cried. "Nothing ever again! I've learned my lesson. I see that, in every fulfillment, there is always a catch. From now on, whether I'm rich or poor, healthy or unhealthy, married or single, whether here on this earth or in the astral plane, I want only my divine Beloved. Wherever God is, there alone lies perfection!"

→2←

Krishna's Cheese

OFTEN, WITH GREAT ENJOYMENT, Yogananda told the following story to illustrate a master's complete lack of ego-consciousness:

"The gopis used to bring fresh cheese every morning to Krishna. Joyfully they would cross the river Jamuna to the other side, where Lord Krishna lived. He relished that cheese because of the devotion with which they brought it.

"One morning, to their great dismay, the river was in flood. How were they to cross it? One of them then had an inspiration.

"Byasa, a great disciple of Krishna's, lived on their own side of the Jamuna. This was the famous Byasa who, years later, wrote the Bhagavad Gita. 'Let us go and plead with him to perform a miracle,' the gopis cried. Eagerly they all rushed to the hut where Byasa lived.

"'Sir,' they cried, 'we've been taking cheese every morning to Lord Krishna. This morning, however, we can't get across: the Jamuna is in flood. Would you please help us?' They smiled at him winningly.

"'Krishna, Krishna!' shouted Byasa as if in anger. 'All I ever hear is "Krishna"! What about me? Does it never occur to you that I, too, might enjoy a little cheese?'

"Well, what a dilemma! They deeply respected Byasa, but this cheese was intended for Krishna. If, however, the only way to get it to him was with Byasa's help, what else could they do? 'Please, Sir,' they said, 'take a little of this cheese for yourself.'

"Well, Byasa took it. And then he ate—and ate—and ate! He didn't stop eating until he couldn't swallow any more. There was only a little portion of cheese left for Krishna! Byasa then hoisted himself to his feet, and somehow carried himself to the riverbank." (Here Yogananda pantomimed lumbering toward the river!)

"'Jamuna!' Byasa cried on reaching the river, 'If I have not eaten anything, divide up and part!'

"'What on earth is he saying?' whispered the girls to one another. 'First he stuffs himself like a pig. And now he cries, "If

I have not eaten." What a liar! What possible good can come of this adventure?'

"To their amazement, the river parted! A narrow opening formed between two great walls of water. The girls crossed hastily to the other side, not stopping to puzzle out this mystery. They hurried to Krishna's cottage, crying out, 'Lord Krishna! Lord Krishna!' Usually, he stood at the cottage door, eagerly awaiting their cheese. Today, however, there was no sign of him. 'Lord Krishna!' they cried, 'Where are you? What's the matter?'

"When they reached his front door, they peeked inside and saw Krishna stretched out on a couch, his mouth curved in a happy smile. To their anxious inquiries, he replied sleepily, 'Oh, I'm sorry, I just can't eat any more cheese today.'

"'But Lord, who fed you? No one else brings you cheese in the morning.'

"'Oh,' he replied, 'that fellow Byasa on the other side has fed me too much already.'

"Byasa, you see, had been thinking only of Krishna as he ate. His body swallowed the cheese, but Krishna got all the benefit.

"Thus," concluded the Master, "should one act in the world. Think always of God. Ask Him, in everything you do, to do it through you."

3

All for a Rag

IN THE DEPTHS OF A JUNGLE in India there lived a holy master and his disciples. Master and disciples woke with the dawn, spreading their prayers with the rising sun. They subsisted on jungle fruits and roots and slept in nature-hewn caves.

Rama had joined this jungle hermitage in order to live a very simple life, but as time went by, he began to find fault with the simple disciplinary duties of the hermitage. One day he said to his guru:

"Honored sir, I am fed up with the day-to-day duties of your hermitage, which are like the worldly duties I performed at home. I want to get away from all materiality and live by myself in solitude in the temple of contemplation."

The master warned him: "Son, you may escape the crowds of people, but it will be more difficult for you to escape your own restless thoughts, which can lead you astray."

Rama paid no heed to the entreaties of his master, and sallied forth in search of a solitary spot. He took with him only two pieces of rag to serve as loincloths, and a begging bowl for water. At last Rama found a very quiet place on top of a hill at the outskirts a local village. He lay down to rest on a rocky ledge under a huge shady tree.

When dawn arrived, young Rama was dismayed to see that a mouse had chewed a few small holes in the second piece of rag, which he had hung on a tree branch. Rama thought, "Heavenly Father, I left all for You, and now you have sent a mouse to work on my last possession—the piece of rag."

A villager passed by the rock and halted to pay respect to the "saint." The villager inquired, "Honored Saint, please tell me what is worrying you." On hearing the story about the chewed rag, the villager advised, "Your Holiness, why don't you keep a cat to frighten away the mice?" "That is a marvelous idea, but where will I get a cat?" asked Rama. "I will bring you a cat tomorrow," replied the villager.

The next day Rama added to his possessions a fuzzy Persian cat. And so the problem of the mice was solved. Every day, Rama went to the village to fetch milk for his cat. The villagers ungrudgingly supplied free milk for the saint's cat for a full year, until one day the village elder said to Rama, "Holy Sir, we are tired of supplying you with milk." "But how is my cat going to live?" retorted Rama. "Why don't you keep a cow?" replied the village headman. "How can I get a cow?"

asked Rama. "I will give you one right now," answered the village elder.

Rama, beside himself with joy, returned to his sylvan home with a cow. Now Rama, the cat, and the cow formed a nice family. This cow was known as the "Saint's Cow" and, like a freeloader, raided the paddy fields of the villagers, causing them extreme anguish.

Another year passed, and many were the tales of the munched paddy fields by the much-tolerated "Saint's Cow." At last one day, the villagers came in a body and complained about the ravages wrought by the audacious cow. "Well, how am I going to feed my cow?" asked Rama. "Why don't you have your own land? We will give you twenty-five acres of land," the villagers said in chorus.

Rama was delighted with this. He gathered together the children of the village, and in the name of God had them build him a cottage-hermitage, till his soil, feed his cat and cow, and do all the hard work required on his farm.

The villagers mutely tolerated all these saintly privileges for two whole years until they found they could not get the children to perform their own duties at home. In a body they went to Rama and complained, "Your Holiness, we have to stop loaning you our children to work on your farm.

Our own farms remain neglected without the help of our children."

"Well, how am I going to manage my farm without the help of your children?" asked Rama.

"Why don't you have your own children? It will be an honor for one of us to give you a marriageable daughter," cried the villagers in unison.

"That is a brilliant idea," cried Rama.

And so Rama was getting ready to be married, when his master came to visit. The master said, "You left the hermitage to get rid of material duties, and now I see you have a cat, a cow, land, a home, and I hear that you are going to get married. What has happened to you?"

"Oh, Master," cried Rama, "This is all for a rag!"

Master and disciple laughed heartily, and Rama left his newly acquired family and farmhouse and returned to live under the wisdom-guidance of his guru's hermitage.

This story illustrates that if you leave the world for God, see that you forsake worldly thoughts *from within*; otherwise, wherever you go, your worldliness will go with you, and attract another worldly environment for you.

4

The Saint Who Chose a King for His Guru

LONG AGO, THERE LIVED A GREAT SAGE named Byasa, the author of the greatest Hindu Scripture, the Bhagavad Gita. He invoked a saintly soul to occupy the body of the baby his wife carried, and taught the unborn child the secrets of the scriptures. This baby was named Sukdeva; by the age of seven he was already versed in all the Hindu scriptures and was ready to renounce the world in search of a true guru.

His father, Byasa, advised him to study with King Janaka, the ruler of that province. As Sukdeva entered the palace grounds, he saw the king sitting on an emerald- and diamond-studded golden throne, smoking a big oriental pipe. This sight was enough for Sukdeva; shocked, he turned and started walking briskly out of the palace gates, muttering to himself, "Shame on my father for sending me to that matter-soaked king. How could he be my teacher?"

But King Janaka was both a king and a saint. Highly advanced spiritually, he knew the thoughts of the fleeing Sukdeva. So, the saint-king sent a messenger to command Sukdeva to return.

Thus, King Janaka and Sukdeva met. The king sent all his courtiers away and, with Sukdeva, entered into an absorbing discourse on the all-protecting God. Four hours passed; Sukdeva was getting hungry and restless, but he dared not disturb the God-intoxicated king.

Another hour passed and two messengers came running to the king, exclaiming, "Your Highness, your kingdom is on fire and the flames threaten to spread to the palace. Won't you come supervise the efforts to extinguish the flames?" To this the king replied, "I am absorbed in discussing the all-protecting God with my friend Sukdeva. I have no time. Go and put out the flames yourselves."

Another hour passed and the same two messengers came running to the King, crying, "Your Royal Excellency, please flee, for the flames have caught the palace on fire and are fast approaching your chamber." To this the king indifferently replied, "Never mind. Don't disturb me, for I am drinking God with my friend. Go, and do the best you can."

Sukdeva was puzzled at the king's reaction. Still another hour passed and two scorched messengers leaped in front of the king, shouting, "Mighty King, behold the flames approaching your throne! Run, before you both are burned to death!" To this the king replied, "You both run, and save yourselves. I am too busy resting in the arms of the all-protecting God to fear any flames."

The messengers fled, and the flames leaped toward the pile of books that Sukdeva had by his side, but the king sat motionless, talking about God.

At last Sukdeva lost his poise and slapped at the flames, trying to prevent them from burning his precious books. The king, satisfied, smilingly waved his hand at the flames and they disappeared at his miraculous touch. Then, as Sukdeva, in great awe, regained his composure and settled down in his seat, the king smilingly spoke.

"O young Sukdeva, you thought of me as a matter-drenched king, but look at yourself. You forsook the all-protecting thought of God to save your pile of books, while I paid no attention to my burning kingdom and palace. God worked this miracle to show that you, though a man of renunciation, are more attached to your books than to God. You are more attached to your books than I am to my kingdom, even though I live in the world instead of in a monastery or hermitage."

This humbled the young Sukdeva, who then took this Saint-King Janaka as his guru, his spiritual teacher.

⇾5⇽

The Mouse Who Became a Tiger

IN A BEAUTIFUL HERMITAGE in the middle of a deep jungle there lived a great, God-realized saint who possessed many miraculous powers. This holy man had no one near to him in this world except a little pet mouse. Many pilgrims and disciples braved the dangers of ferocious tigers and wild beasts of the forest in order to visit the great saint, and all brought offerings of fruits and flowers. Everyone who came to visit the saint marveled at the great friendship between him and the mouse. He was known as the "Saint's Mouse," and everybody threw tidbits to him.

One day, when a group of students were visiting the great master, the mouse came running in chased by a cat. As the mouse sought refuge at the feet of the master, the saint—before the wondering gaze of his students—changed the little mouse into a huge, ferocious cat. The metamorphosed mouse was happy now, safe from cats, and only resented it when some of the disciples would exclaim, "Oh, look at the saint's glorified mouse-cat."

One day, while the same students were visiting the master, the cat, pursued by jungle dogs, came racing in at top speed for protection at the feet of the sage. The sage exclaimed, "From now on, be thou a wild dog." In that moment, to the surprise of the wild dogs, the mouse-cat changed into a dog.

Sometime later, while the students were studying with the master, a full-grown Royal Bengal tiger chased the mouse-dog into the hermitage. The master exclaimed: "Mr. Mouse, I am sick of constantly protecting you from your enemies, so you must be a tiger henceforth."

No sooner had the saint said this than the mouse-dog became transformed into a huge Bengal tiger. The students laughed heartily, exclaiming, "Look at that saint's wild tiger. He is only a glorified mouse." As days went by, first-time visitors discovered a fearsome tiger patrolling the hermitage grounds. If these guests were frightened, some students would say sarcastically, "Don't be nervous. That is not a tiger. It is only a mouse glorified into a tiger by the master."

The mouse-tiger got tired of being constantly belittled in this way, so he thought, "If only I could get rid of the saint, then the constant memory of my origin as a mouse could be removed." Thinking this, the mouse-tiger sprang to kill the master, to the great consternation of his disciples.

Beholding the ungrateful motive of his transformed pet, in that instant the sage loudly commanded, "Be thou a mouse again," and lo, the roaring tiger was transformed into a squeaking little mouse.

Now remember, dear friends, many of you have used God-given will power to change from a little human mouse, squeaking with failure and fear, into a brave tiger of industry and power. But do not forget that if you are antagonistic to that power, you may change again from a tiger of power to a mouse of failure. So never forget God while you perform your duties, and always, in the background of your mind, hum a silent devotional song of love to your beloved Heavenly Father.

→6←

How a Saint Converted a Thief

TULSIDAS, A PIOUS SAINT, used to worship God in the form of Rama, the great prophet of India. Wealthy devotees of Tulsidas, inspired by his intense devotion, gave him many gold utensils to be used in his sacred temple ceremonies. Tulsidas, while he meditated deeply on Rama, noticed an underlying fear that these gold utensils would be stolen.

His fear was not unfounded, for a thief had learned about the temple's gold utensils. Saint Tulsidas left the temple open, and at night he used to meditate under a bower of fragrant flowers, about one hundred yards from the temple. The thief planned to go there at night and steal the utensils, but for seven nights as he approached the temple, he beheld the living image of the prophet Rama guarding the temple entrance.

Bewildered, the thief dressed himself up as a gentleman and went to Tulsidas one morning, saying, "Honored Sir, I have heard that you do not lock the temple door even at night, for you always invite true devotees to meditate there. Yet for seven nights I have wanted to enter your temple to meditate and receive the holy vibrations, but I dared not enter because your sentry, dressed as Prophet Rama and equipped with bow and arrows, was menacingly guarding the temple door."

Tulsidas, with tears in his eyes, asked the gentleman, "Is it true that you saw Rama guarding the temple door? Well, sir, I'm sorry. I will ask my sentry not to guard the temple door any more, so that you can visit the temple at any time."

Tulsidas realized that this "gentleman" was really a thief. But he also realized that his fear of losing the gold utensils had attracted the prophet Rama to materialize and lovingly guard the temple treasures for him.

The saint retired to the temple and meditated all day long, praying to Rama, "Lord, please take away my gold utensils. I'm ashamed to have bothered you with my fears and caused you to be awake through the night guarding the temple utensils. Please desist from assuming the part of my sentry." Rama appeared in a vision and smilingly agreed to the prayer of his devotee.

That night the thief, making sure that Tulsidas was deeply meditating under his favorite tree, once again crept silently through the garden. As Tulsidas had promised, there was no divine guard at the temple entrance. On tiptoe the thief stole into the temple, hurriedly gathered most of the golden utensils in his gunnysack, and then quickly left the temple. At that point, a stray dog began to howl and chase him. The thief, with the golden utensils tinkling in the gunnysack, now chased by the barking dog, broke into a run.

Tulsidas, having finished his meditation, was resting under the tree and expecting the return of the thief. When he heard the howling dog, the racing feet, and the tinkling sound of the gold utensils, he went into the temple and discovered the loss of almost all of the utensils.

Hurriedly gathering up the remaining few gold pieces, Tulsidas tied them in a napkin, and raced in the direction of the barking dog. He quickly overtook the thief, who, in remorse and almost beside himself with fear, fell at the feet of the saint and cried, "Gracious Saint, please take back your gold utensils. I beg you not to turn me over to the police."

The saint laughed merrily and, patting the thief on the back, handed him the rest of the gold utensils, saying, "Son, I did not overtake you to arrest you, but only to give you the rest of the utensils, which in your hurry you missed. I am glad to be relieved of them, for they distracted me from my meditation on my beloved Rama. Son, you need them more than I do. Take them all with my blessing. However, the next time you want anything from the temple, please don't steal it and poison your spiritual life. Just ask me and I will willingly give it to you."

The thief was dumbfounded at the astounding nonattachment, devotion, forgiveness, and generosity of Tulsidas, and, bowing deeply before him, held the saint's feet tightly to his bosom, talking amidst sobs, "Honored Saint, I am a thief by profession, but I have never met a greater thief than you. Today, you have stolen everything from me—my body, mind, desires, aspirations, heart, and my very soul, as well as the gold utensils that you gave me. I don't want to be a thief of perishable articles any longer, but I want to be a thief of souls like you."

Saying this, the thief, now a disciple, followed the master to the temple, and ever after they walked, dreamed, and loved God together.

The above story illustrates that the love of God must be supreme. You must discard desires for perishable things. This will not make you negative and joyless, but instead will bring the imperishable, ever-new, ever-increasing joy of God.

APPENDICES

Appendix 1: Stories and Humorous Passages

All for a Rag 128–31
"Any old fish can float downstream." 49
The Bad Man Who Was Preferred by God 74–79
Bernard and the Turban 109
The Big Frog and the Little Frog 63–64
Billy Sunday and St. Peter 71
The Buckshot of Smiles 44
Cheese for Krishna 125–27
Cleaning Up After Yogananda 118–19
Crabbiness and Sweetness 43
The Cure for a Nervous Heart 52–53
Different Kinds of Craziness 17–18
The Egotist Makes Much Noise 60
Energization Exercises and the Policeman 113–14
Father Divine 30
The Fiery Oven for a Farmer's Son 19–21
"Gimme a dime." 104–5
The "Hangman's Dinner" 58
A Hindu Priest Leads Followers to Heaven 22–25
How a Saint Converted a Thief 137–41
A Hundred-dollar Bill in the Collection Plate 70–71
"I thought you were the wall." 34
The Irishman, Englishman, and Scotsman 29
A Lady Tries to Meditate 83–86
"Let the mountain be removed and cast into the sea." 69
The Lion Who Became a Sheep 92–95
The Magic Carrot 64–66
The Man Who Became a Buffalo 89–91
The Man Who Refused Heaven 44–45
The Master Never Sleeps 116–17
The Miracle Man 71–73
Mistaken Identity—Semi-Developed Intuition 61–62
"Mr. Roquefort" 54
Money for Ice Cream 111–12

"Monkey Consciousness" 87–89
The Mouse Who Became a Tiger 135–37
A New Cement Floor 99–100
The Nuns and Watermelon 110
"On top of the dome of the Taj Mahal!" 31–32
"Only your blessing is lacking!" 112
The Over-Taxed "Public Servant"—Digestion 51–52
The Philosopher and the Boatman 34–36
Playing Dead 100
Portrait of a Businessman 59–60
A Pretty Shade of Lipstick and a Smart-Looking Tie 43
Race Prejudice and the Negro Janitor 21–22
Rasheed's Pranks 101–2
Reincarnation in a Nutshell 123–25
A Robe and Long Hair 102–3
Saint Teresa of Avila, Friend of Jesus 70
The Saint Who Chose a King for His Guru 132–34
Samadhi at the Movies and on the Subway 106
"Shay, whad're you drink'n'?" 41
"She is my soul mate." 42–43
Six Burly Policeman Sent Tumbling 105–6
A Six-Inch Tongue 43
Sub Gum Duff 114–16
The Two Sleeping Boys 39–40
Two Toy Guns 110–11
A Vacuum Cleaner and Meditation 83
"Where is the oil?" 32–34
"Why don't we use the word service?" 117–18
Women Are More Influenced by Feeling 40–41
"Won't power" 52
The "Worry Fast" 49–51
Yogananda's Infectious Laughter 30
You Don't Have to Own a Thing to Enjoy It 103
"You forgot to take the hat!" 57–58
"You will go to hell." 18
Your Bank of Happiness 58–59
"Your teeth are like stars." 29

Appendix 2: Resources

BOOKS BY SWAMI KRIYANANDA THAT SHARE QUOTATIONS AND STORIES FROM HIS LIFE WITH PARAMHANSA YOGANANDA

- **Conversations with Yogananda**

- **The Essence of Self-Realization**

- **The New Path:**
  My Life with Paramhansa Yogananda

- **Paramhansa Yogananda:**
  A Biography with Personal Reflections and Reminiscences

All published by Crystal Clarity Publishers. (See pages 154–56.)

About the Authors

Paramhansa Yogananda

"As a bright light shining in the midst of darkness, so was Yogananda's presence in this world. Such a great soul comes on earth only rarely, when there is a real need among men."

—The Shankaracharya of Kanchipuram

Born in India in 1893, Paramhansa Yogananda was trained from his early years to bring India's ancient science of Self-realization to the West. In 1920 he moved to the United States to begin what was to develop into a worldwide work touching millions of lives. Americans were hungry for India's spiritual teachings, and for the liberating techniques of yoga.

In 1946 he published what has become a spiritual classic and one of the best-loved books of the twentieth century, *Autobiography of a Yogi*. In addition, Yogananda established headquarters for a worldwide work, wrote a number of books and study courses, gave lectures to thousands in most major cities across the United States, wrote music and poetry, and trained disciples. He was invited to the White House by Calvin Coolidge, and he initiated Mahatma Gandhi into Kriya Yoga, his most advanced meditation technique.

Yogananda's message to the West highlighted the unity of all religions, and the importance of love for God combined with scientific techniques of meditation.

Swami Kriyananda

"Swami Kriyananda is a man of wisdom and compassion in action, truly one of the leading lights in the spiritual world today."

—Lama Surya Das, Dzogchen Center,
author of *Awakening the Buddha Within*

A prolific author and composer, and a world-renowned spiritual teacher, **Swami Kriyananda** (1926–2013) referred to himself simply as a humble disciple of the great God-realized master, Paramhansa Yogananda. He met his guru at the young age of twenty-two, and served him during the last four years of the Master's life. He dedicated the rest of his life to sharing Yogananda's teachings throughout the world.

During a period of intense inward reflection, he discovered Yogananda's *Autobiography of a Yogi*, and immediately traveled three thousand miles to meet the Master, who accepted him as a monastic disciple. Yogananda appointed him as the head of the monastery, authorized him to teach in his name and to give initiation into Kriya Yoga, and entrusted him with the missions of writing and developing what he called "world brotherhood colonies."

Recognized as the "father of the spiritual communities movement," Swami Kriyananda founded Ananda World Brotherhood Community in the Sierra Nevada foothills of Northern California in 1968. It has served as a model for eight communities founded subsequently in the United States, Europe, and India.

Expanding the Light

ANANDA SANGHA WORLDWIDE

Ananda Sangha is a fellowship of kindred souls following the teachings of Paramhansa Yogananda. The Sangha embraces the search for higher consciousness through the practice of meditation, and through the ideal of service to others in their quest for Self-realization. Approximately ten thousand spiritual seekers are affiliated with Ananda Sangha throughout the world.

Founded in 1968 by Swami Kriyananda, a direct disciple of Paramhansa Yogananda, Ananda includes seven communities in the United States, Europe, and in India. Worldwide, about one thousand devotees live in these spiritual communities, which are based on Yogananda's ideals of "plain living and high thinking."

Swami Kriyananda lived with his guru during the last four years of the Master's life, and continued to serve his organization for another ten years, bringing the teachings of Kriya Yoga and Self-realization to audiences in the United States, Europe, Australia, and, from 1958–1962, India. In 1968, together with a small group of close friends and students, he founded the first "world-brotherhood community" in the foothills of the Sierra Nevada Mountains in northeastern California. Initially a meditation retreat center located on sixty-seven acres of forested land, Ananda World-Brotherhood Community today encompasses one thousand acres where about 250 people live a dynamic, fulfilling life based on the principles and practices of spiritual, mental, and physical development, cooperation, respect, and divine friendship.

At this printing, after forty years of existence, Ananda is one of the most successful networks of intentional communities in the world. Urban communities have been developed in Palo Alto and Sacramento, California; Portland, Oregon; and Seattle, Washington. In Europe, near Assisi, Italy, a spiritual retreat and community was established in 1983, where today nearly one hundred residents from eight countries live. And in India, new communities have been founded in Gurgaon (near New Delhi) and in Pune.

THE EXPANDING LIGHT

We are visited by over two thousand people each year. Offering a varied, year-round schedule of classes and workshops on yoga, meditation, spiritual practices, yoga and meditation teacher training, and personal renewal retreats, The Expanding Light welcomes seekers from all backgrounds. Here you will find a loving, accepting environment, ideal for personal growth and spiritual renewal.

We strive to create an ideal relaxing and supportive environment for people to explore their own spiritual growth. We share the nonsectarian meditation practices and yoga philosophy of Paramhansa Yogananda and his direct disciple, Ananda's founder, Swami Kriyananda. Yogananda called his path "Self-realization," and our goal is to help our guests tune in to their own higher Selves.

Guests at The Expanding Light can learn the four practices that comprise Yogananda's teachings of Kriya Yoga: the Energization Exercises, the *Hong Sau* technique of concentration, the AUM technique, and Kriya Yoga. The first two techniques are available for all guests; the second two are available to those interested in pursuing this path more deeply.

CRYSTAL CLARITY PUBLISHERS

When you're seeking a book on practical spiritual living, you want to know it's based on an authentic tradition of timeless teachings, and that it resonates with integrity. This is the goal of Crystal Clarity Publishers: to offer you books of practical wisdom filled with true spiritual principles that have not only been tested through the ages, but also through personal experience.

We publish only books that combine creative thinking, universal principles, and a timeless message. Crystal Clarity books will open doors to help you discover more fulfillment and joy by living and acting from the center of peace within you.

Crystal Clarity Publishers—recognized worldwide for its bestselling, original, unaltered edition of Paramhansa Yogananda's classic *Autobiography of a Yogi*—offers many additional resources to assist you in your spiritual journey, including over one hundred books, a wide variety of inspirational and relaxation music composed by Swami Kriyananda (Yogananda's direct disciple), and yoga and meditation DVDs.

For our online catalog, complete with secure ordering, please visit us on the web at: **WWW.CRYSTALCLARITY.COM**

Crystal Clarity music and audiobooks are available on all the popular online download sites. Look for us on your favorite online music website.

To request a catalog, place an order for the products you read about in the Further Explorations section of this book, or to find out more information about us and our products, please contact us:

Contact Information for Ananda Sangha Worldwide

mail: 14618 Tyler Foote Road • Nevada City, CA 95959
phone: 530.478.7560
online: www.ananda.org / sanghainfo@ananda.org

Contact Information the Expanding Light

mail: 14618 Tyler Foote Road • Nevada City, CA 95959
phone: 800.346.5350
online: www.expandinglight.org / info@expandinglight.org

Contact Information for Crystal Clarity Publishers

mail: 14618 Tyler Foote Road • Nevada City, CA 95959
phone: 800.424.1055 *or* 530.478.7600
online: www.crystalclarity.com / clarity@crystalclarity.com

Further Explorations

If you are inspired by this book and would like to learn more about Yogananda's teachings, we offer many additional resources:

Crystal Clarity publishes the original 1946, unedited edition of Paramhansa Yogananda's spiritual masterpiece

Autobiography of a Yogi
Paramhansa Yogananda

One of the best-selling Eastern philosophy titles of all time, with millions of copies sold, this book was named one of the best and most influential books of the twentieth century. This highly prized reprinting of the original 1946 edition is the only one available free from textual changes made after Yogananda's death.

In this updated edition are bonus materials, including a last chapter that Yogananda wrote in 1951, without posthumous changes, the eulogy that Yogananda wrote for Gandhi, and a new foreword and afterword by Swami Kriyananda, one of Yogananda's close, direct disciples.

PRAISE FOR *Autobiography of a Yogi*

"In the original edition, published during Yogananda's life, one is more in contact with Yogananda himself." —*David Frawley, Director, American Institute of Vedic Studies, author of* Yoga and Ayurveda

ALSO AVAILABLE AS AN **UNABRIDGED AUDIOBOOK IN MP3 FORMAT**

Crystal Clarity is also pleased to offer these two biographies of Paramhansa Yogananda by his direct disciple, Swami Kriyananda.

Paramhansa Yogananda
A Biography with Personal Reflections and Reminiscences
Swami Kriyananda

Taking up where Yogananda's celebrated *Autobiography of a Yogi* leaves off., this book will thrill the millions of readers of Yogananda's autobiography with scores of new stories from Yogananda's life—some charmingly human, some deeply inspiring, and many recounting miracles equal to those of the Bible. These stories are told from firsthand experience, and bring the Master alive unlike any other book ever written about him.

Now, Swami Kriyananda brilliantly puts to rest many misconceptions about his great guru, and reveals Yogananda's many-sided greatness. The author's profound grasp of the purpose of Yogananda's life, his inner nature, and his plans for the future are revelatory and sublime. Included is an insider's portrait of the great teacher's last years. More than a factual biography, this book also outlines the great master's key teachings.

Feel the power of Paramhansa Yogananda's divine consciousness and his impact on the world as presented with clarity and love by one of his few remaining direct disciples.

The New Path
My Life with Paramhansa Yogananda
Swami Kriyananda

This is the moving story of Kriyananda's years with Paramhansa Yogananda, India's emissary to the West and the first yoga master to spend the greater part of his life in America.

When Swami Kriyananda discovered *Autobiography of a Yogi* in 1948, he was totally new to Eastern teachings. This is a great advantage to the Western reader, since Kriyananda walks us along the yogic path as he discovers it from the moment of his initiation as a disciple of Yogananda. With winning honesty, humor, and deep insight, he shares his journey along the spiritual path through personal stories and experiences.

Praise for *The New Path*

"Reading *Autobiography of a Yogi* by Yogananda was a transformative experience for me and for millions of others. In *The New Path* . . . Swami Kriyananda carries on this great tradition. Highly recommended." —*Dean Ornish, MD, Founder and President, Preventative Medicine Research Institute, Clinical Professor of Medicine, University of California, San Francisco, author of* The Spectrum

"Required reading for every spiritual seeker. I heartily recommend it." — *Michael Toms, Founder, New Dimensions Media, and author of* An Open Life: Joseph Campbell in Conversation with Michael Toms

ALSO AVAILABLE AS AN **UNABRIDGED AUDIOBOOK IN MP3 FORMAT**

The Essence of Self-Realization
The Wisdom of Paramhansa Yogananda
Recorded, Compiled, & Edited by His Disciple, Swami Kriyananda

With nearly three hundred sayings rich with spiritual wisdom, this book is the fruit of a labor of love. A glance at the table of contents will convince the reader of the vast scope of this book. It offers as complete an explanation of life's true purpose, and of the way to achieve that purpose, as may be found anywhere.

"Self-realization is the knowing in all parts of body, mind, and soul that you are now in possession of the kingdom of God ... that God's omnipresence is your omnipresence; and that all that you need to do is improve your knowing."
–Swami Kriyananda, from the book

Conversations with Yogananda
Edited with commentary by Swami Kriyananda

This is an unparalleled, first-hand account of the teachings of Paramhansa Yogananda. Featuring nearly 500 never-before-released stories, sayings, and insights, this is an extensive, yet eminently accessible, fund of wisdom from one of the twentieth century's most famous yoga masters. Compiled and edited with commentary by Swami Kriyananda, one of Yogananda's closest direct disciples.

"This book is a treasure trove. If your goal is to grow spiritually, get a copy now." —*Richard Salva, author of* Walking with William of Normandy: A Paramhansa Yogananda Pilgrimage Guide

The Essence of the Bhagavad Gita
Explained by Paramhansa Yogananda
As Remembered by His Disciple, Swami Kriyananda

Rarely in a lifetime does a new spiritual classic appear that has the power to change people's lives and transform future generations. This is such a book.

This revelation of India's best-loved scripture approaches it from a fresh perspective, showing its deep allegorical meaning and its down-to-earth practicality. The themes presented are universal: how to achieve victory in life in union with the divine; how to prepare for life's "final exam," death, and what happens afterward; and, how to triumph over all pain and suffering.

PRAISE FOR *The Essence of the Bhagavad Gita*

"A brilliant text that will greatly enhance the spiritual life of every reader."
—*Caroline Myss, author of* Anatomy of the Spirit *and* Sacred Contracts

"It is doubtful that there has been a more important spiritual writing in the last fifty years than this soul-stirring, monumental work. What a gift! What a treasure!" —*Neale Donald Walsch, author of* Conversations with God

"I loved reading this!" —*Fred Alan Wolf, Ph.D., physicist, aka Dr. Quantum, author of* Dr. Quantum's Little Book of Big Ideas *and* The Yoga of Time Travel

"It has the power to change your life." —*Bernie Siegel, MD, author of* 101 Exercises for the Soul *and* Love, Medicine and Miracles!

ALSO AVAILABLE AS AN **UNABRIDGED AUDIOBOOK IN MP3 FORMAT**
AND AS **PAPERBACK WITHOUT COMMENTARY**: *THE BHAGAVAD GITA*

Whispers from Eternity
Paramhansa Yogananda
Edited by His Disciple, Swami Kriyananda

Yogananda was not only a spiritual master, but a master poet, whose poems revealed the hidden divine presence behind even everyday things.

Open this book, pick a poem at random, and read it. Mentally repeat whatever phrase appeals to you. Within a short time, you will feel your consciousness transformed. This book has the power to rapidly accelerate your spiritual growth, and provides hundreds of delightful ways for you to begin your own conversation with God.

ALSO AVAILABLE AS AN **UNABRIDGED AUDIOBOOK IN MP3 FORMAT**

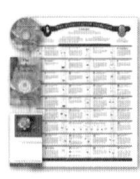

Energization Exercises
Paramhansa Yogananda, Swami Kriyananda. and others

The *Energization Exercises*, as taught in the Ananda Course in Self-Realization, are a wonderful system of exercises originated by Paramhansa Yogananda. Best learned at Ananda, they are also taught here in a variety of formats.

Based on ancient teachings and eternal realities, Yogananda explains that the whole physical universe, including man, is surrounded by, and made of cosmic energy. Through daily use of these exercises we can systematically recharge our bodies with greater energy and train our minds to understand the true source of that power.

AVAILABLE IN **DVD, BOOKLET, BOOK. AND INSTRUCTIONAL CD**

Crystal Clarity is also pleased to offer an important series of scriptural interpretations based on the teachings of Paramhansa Yogananda.

Revelations of Christ
Proclaimed by Paramhansa Yogananda,
Presented by His Disciple, Swami Kriyananda

Over the past years, our faith has been severely shaken by experiences such as the breakdown of church authority, discoveries of ancient texts that supposedly contradict long-held beliefs, and the sometimes outlandish historical analyses of Scripture by academics. Together, these forces have helped create confusion and uncertainty about the true teachings and meanings of Christ's life.

This soul-stirring book, presenting the teachings of Christ from the experience and perspective of Yogananda, finally offers the fresh understanding of Christ's teachings for which the world has been waiting, in a more reliable way than any other: by learning from those saints who have communed directly, in deep ecstasy, with Christ and God.

PRAISE FOR *Revelations of Christ*

"This is a great gift to humanity. It is a spiritual treasure to cherish and to pass on to children for generations. This remarkable and magnificent book brings us to the doorway of a deeper, richer embracing of Eternal Truth." —*Neale Donald Walsch, author of* Conversations with God

ALSO AVAILABLE AS AN **UNABRIDGED AUDIOBOOK IN MP3 FORMAT**

Demystifying Patanjali,
The Yoga Sutras (Aphorisms)
The Wisdom of Yogananda
Swami Kriyananda

About 2200 years ago, a great spiritual master of India named Patanjali presented humanity with a step-by-step outline of how all truth seekers and saints achieve divine union. He called this universal inner experience and process "yoga" or "union." Now, a modern yoga master—Paramhansa Yogananda—has resurrected Patanjali's original revelations, and here Swami Kriyananda shares Yogananda's crystal clear explanations.

THE WISDOM OF YOGANANDA SERIES

This series features writings of Paramhansa Yogananda not available elsewhere. Included are writings from his earliest years in America, in an approachable, easy-to-read format and presented with minimal editing, to capture his expansive and compassionate wisdom, his sense of fun, and his practical spiritual guidance.

How to Be Happy All the Time
The Wisdom of Yogananda Series, Volume 1
Paramhansa Yogananda

Yogananda powerfully explains everything needed to lead a happier, more fulfilling life. Topics include: looking for happiness in the right places; choosing to be happy; tools and techniques for achieving happiness; sharing happiness with others; and balancing success and happiness.

Karma and Reincarnation
The Wisdom of Yogananda Series, Volume 2
Paramhansa Yogananda

Yogananda reveals the truth behind karma, death, reincarnation, and the afterlife. With clarity and simplicity, he makes the mysterious understandable. Topics include: why we see a world of suffering and inequality; how to handle the challenges in our lives; what happens at death, and after death; and the origin and purpose of reincarnation.

Spiritual Relationships
The Wisdom of Yogananda Series, Volume 3
Paramhansa Yogananda

This book contains practical guidance and fresh insight on relationships of all types. Topics include: how to cure bad habits that can end true friendship; how to choose the right partner and create a lasting marriage; sex in marriage and how to conceive a spiritual child; problems that arise in marriage and what to do about them; the Universal Love behind all your relationships, and many more.

"[A] thoroughly 'user friendly' guide on how yoga principles can actually help relationships grow and thrive. Yogananda's keys to understanding yoga's underlying philosophy [teach] how to cure bad habits, expand love boundaries, and understand relationship problems."

—*James A. Cox, Chief Editor,* The Bookwatch

How to Be a Success
The Wisdom of Yogananda Series, Volume 4
Paramhansa Yogananda

This book includes the complete text of *The Attributes of Success*, the original booklet later published as *The Law of Success*. In addition, you will learn how to find your purpose in life, develop habits of success and eradicate habits of failure, develop your will power and magnetism, and thrive in the right job.

Winner of the 2011 International Book Award for the Best Self-Help Book of the Year

How to Have Courage, Calmness and Confidence
The Wisdom of Yogananda Series, Volume 5
Paramhansa Yogananda

Everyone can be courageous, calm, and confident, because these are qualities of the soul. Hypnotized with material thinking and desires, many of us have lost touch with our inner power. In this potent book of spiritual wisdom, Paramhansa Yogananda shares the most effective steps for reconnecting with your divine nature.

The Essence of Self-Realization
The Wisdom of Yogananda Series, Volume 6
*Recorded, Compiled, & Edited by His Disciple,
  Swami Kriyananda*

Paramhansa Yogananda, a foremost spiritual teacher of modern times, offers practical, wide-ranging, and fascinating suggestions on how to have more energy and to live a radiantly healthy life. The principles in this book promote physical health and all-round well-being, mental clarity, and ease and inspiration in your spiritual life.

Readers will discover • Priceless Energization Exercises for rejuvenating the body and mind • The art of conscious relaxation • Diet tips for health and beauty.

How to Awaken Your True Potential
The Wisdom of Yogananda Series, Volume 7
Paramhansa Yogananda

Every soul is on a journey of self-discovery, the length of the journey depends on the choices we make. In this inspiring book, Yogananda instructs you how to: • Shake old, limiting habits and attitudes • Cultivate new positive habits • Use the tremendous power of your mind • Understand the benefits of meditation • Live your true potentiald well-being, mental clarity, and ease and inspiration in your spiritual life.

Music and Audiobooks

We offer many of our book titles in unabridged MP3 format audiobooks. To purchase these titles and to see more music and audiobook offerings, visit our website: www.crystalclarity.com. Or look for us in the popular online download sites.

Metaphysical Meditations
Swami Kriyananda

Kriyananda's soothing voice guides you in thirteen different meditations based on the soul-inspiring, mystical poetry of Yogananda. Each meditation is accompanied by beautiful classical music to help you quiet your thoughts and prepare for deep states of meditation. Includes a full recitation of Yogananda's poem "Samadhi." A great aid to the serious meditator, as well as to those just beginning their practice.

Relax: Meditations for Flute and Cello
Donald Walters
Featuring David Eby and Sharon Nani

This CD is specifically designed to slow respiration and heart rate, bringing listeners to their calm center. This recording features fifteen melodies for flute and cello, accompanied by harp, guitar, keyboard, and strings. Excellent for creating a calming atmosphere for work and home.

AUM: Mantra of Eternity
Swami Kriyananda

This recording features nearly seventy minutes of continuous vocal chanting of AUM, the Sanskrit word meaning peace and oneness of spirit, as extensively discussed by Yogananda in *Autobiography of a Yogi*. By attuning one's consciousness to this sound, one enters the stream of vibration that proceeded out of Spirit, and that emerges back into the Spirit at creation's end and at the end of the individual soul's cycle of outward wandering. By merging in AUM, liberation is attained.

OTHER TITLES IN THE MANTRA SERIES:
Gayatri Mantra ❀ *Mahamrityanjaya Mantra* ❀ *Maha Mantra*

Bliss Chants
Ananda Kirtan

Chanting focuses and lifts the mind to higher states of consciousness. *Bliss Chants* features chants written by Yogananda and his direct disciple, Swami Kriyananda. They're performed by Ananda Kirtan, a group of singers and musicians from Ananda, one of the world's most respected yoga communities. Chanting is accompanied by guitar, harmonium, kirtals, and tabla.

OTHER TITLES IN THE CHANT SERIES:
Divine Mother Chants ❀ *Power Chants* ❀ *Love Chants*
Peace Chants ❀ *Wisdom Chants* ❀ *Wellness Chants*

More Crystal Clarity Titles

Also from Crystal Clarity Publishers, some of our popular books

---

Demystifying Patanjali

The Meaning of Dreaming

The Rubaiyat of Omar Khayyam

Intuition for Starters

Chakras for Starters

The Art and Science of Raja Yoga

Awaken to Superconsciousness

Meditation for Starters *with CD*

Self-Expansion Through Marriage

Change Your Magnetism, Change Your Life

The Yugas

A Tale of Songs

The Harmonium Handbook

The Art of Supportive Leadership

Money Magnetism

The Need for Spiritual Communities

The Yoga of Abraham Lincoln

Awaken to Superconsciousness

The Healing Kitchen

Education for Life

How to Meditate

Touch of Light

Love Perfected, Life Divine

Sharing Nature

The Sky and Earth Touched Me

Listening to Nature

For our online catalog, visit **www.crystalclarity.com**